The Gift of Love

The Gift of LOVE

R. L. Middleton

Broadman Press/Nashville, Tennessee

1976

© Copyright 1976 • Broadman Press

All rights reserved

4251-45 (Trade Edition)

ISBN: 0-8054-5145-5 (Trade Edition)

4282-44 (BRP Edition)

Dewey Decimal Classification: 242

Subject Headings: LOVE // MEDITATION

Library of Congress Catalog Card Number: 76-2241

Printed in the United States of America

This volume is affectionately dedicated
to our grandchildren
Lee Moench Gant
William Lynn Moench, Jr.
Robert Waide Moench
David Edwards Moench
all of whom know the meaning
of God's love and unselfishly share it
with others

CONTENTS

The material in this book has been collected over a long period of time. Many of the original sources are unknown to the author, but every possible effort has been made to give proper credit and to secure permission from the original author or publisher. Any omission of credit is unintentional. It is my hope and prayer that the reader will be blessed in his devotional life as my thoughts are shared with him and others.

R. L. Middleton

Nashville, Tennessee

"Whoso hath the world's good, and seeth his brother have need, and shutteth up his bowels of compassion from him, how dwelleth the love of God in him? My little children, let us not love in word, neither in tongue; but in deed and in truth" (1 John 3:17-18).

1. The Jericho Road

The lesson of the Good Samaritan is, unquestionably, along with that of the Prodigal Son, one of the most familiar and beloved lessons our Savior taught. It has been woven into humanitarian and charitable appeals without number. He is telling of a journey of mercy with a spiritual purpose in mind, and we should not miss this fact.

On the other hand, the story of the Prodigal Son brings into focus the forgiving love of God, as the old father continues to look down the road for the return of his wayward son. This is a vivid picture of our Savior and his compassion on us; no matter how far away one may wander away in sin, he is always ready to welcome us back and to forgive. I can never get over the wonderful way our Lord can transform the life of a sinner and can give meaning to a shallow, foolish, and frivolous life, as he pours in the oil and wine of his Spirit and his Word.

First, may we notice that the kindness of the Samaritan was something which sprang spontaneously from the heart, not something which was done out of a feeling of duty and obligation. In other words, it was not by law, but by love. The man en route to Jericho was attacked and robbed by thieves. Then, he was left alone by his fellow Israelites, the priest and the Levite. It was a despised Samaritan, to whom he would have looked for nothing, who came as his deliverer.

There are two sides to the story, the positive and the negative. Unfortunately, the negative side is predominant in our daily news reports. We seldom hear of an act such as was displayed by the Samaritan. The lack of God's love in today's world is shocking.

More than forty years ago, a student at Randolph-Macon College preserved for us the account of an unusual chapel service conducted during his college days. It was a service long to be remembered and from which there are many thought provoking lessons.

"Perhaps the most highly respected and appreciated member of the faculty, the college dean, not only for his scholarship; but also for his noble living and friendly counsel, Dr. Hall Canter, was the speaker. He read the story of the Good Samaritan, as recorded in the tenth chapter of Luke's gospel. He read it carefully, distinctly, and with much feeling. Then he closed the Bible. After a moment, he said. 'Young gentlemen, that road from Jerusalem to Jericho runs right through your dormitory. Chapel dismissed.'

"The students were stunned. The service was over in less than five minutes, but most of them never forgot that morning or the message."[1]

One has to wonder why this man of God made that statement. Had some situation arisen in the school or in the community? Had some member of the faculty or the student body suffered reverses or some calamity deserving of mercy and compassion, as was demonstrated by the Good Samaritan on the Jericho Road?

One simply does not know. But Dr. Canter had a good

reason to remind them of their duty and obligation to do good and to show love for their fellowman at every opportunity. There are two sides to the story—the positive and the negative. The robbers and the two men who passed by on the other side"—and the Good Samaritan and his demonstration of love and mercy for the beaten and wounded traveler. The negative side seems to be predominating all across the world. Individuals are being robbed, murdered, raped, cars are being stolen, homes are being broken into. You name it! Department stores lose millions of dollars worth of merchandise by shoplifters—all the victims of travelers on the Jericho Road of business and commerce. Law enforcement officers and the courts seen unable to do much about it.

Here in our community of Nashville, Tennessee, during a period of less than thirty days in February and March, 1975, there occured crimes of almost every nature, some of them too terrible to report. They have been distressing, nauseating horrible beyond description, but they are the facts of life.

February 10, 1975, our morning paper carried the story of the death of a nineteen-year-old university freshman who had been raped and murdered in her apartment less than a block from the campus. The case has never been solved.

Exactly one week later, just before daylight, a burly man found his way into a girl's dormitory of another college. Trying the doors to all of the rooms until he found one unlocked, he slipped in and awakened a young lady with a knife at her throat. After raping her three times, he slipped out of the building and into the early morning darkness. The victim dared not scream or else she might have been killed. Fortunately, thirty days later the rapist was caught breaking into the workshop of an apartment building. The police found jewelry on him belonging to the young lady. With this evidence, he confessed. He is still awaiting trial.

Both of these accounts of crime are tragic, but when a child is involved, it is even more heartbreaking. Here is what happened ten days after these two other crimes.

The Girl Scout cookie sale was in full swing. Nine-year-old, blue-eyed Marcia Trimble had about completed her quota. As darkness began to settle over her neighborhood, she said to her mother, "Mama, I am going across the street to carry the cookies to Mrs. Maxwell. I'll be right back." She never arrived. She never returned home, apparently a kidnap victim, yet no ransom note was ever received.

As news spread over the city by radio and television, police and hundreds of volunteers began an all-night search. This continued for days and on into weeks without results.

On Easter Sunday morning, thirty-three days after Marcia's disappearance, a house guest of a family which lives on an adjoining street went out to the garage in search of a cover for a fishing boat motor he had purchased. In his search, he noticed a child's foot protruding from under a small plastic wading pool. Further investigation revealed Marcia's body, along with a carton containing several boxes of unsold cookies, together with an empty envelope which had contained $10 or $12, the proceeds of cookies sold.

Unbelievable! Yes, that garage, located less than 200

yards from the Trimble home, had been searched many times by various individuals during the weeks which had elapsed. Where had this precious child been for thirty-three days is still an unanswered question.

A medical examiner's decision was that Marcia had been manually strangled only a few days before her body was found. He further ruled that since deterioration was meager, her body had been placed in the garage only one or two nights previously.

This horrible crime is still unsolved. Was it for robbery or the work of a dope addict? She had not been sexually molested. Just another victim of travelers on the Jericho road which runs through every neighborhood, every school, business, and through society.

I recognize that all these are morbid stories, but they are stark realities. What is the answer to all such crimes?

The Sunday after Marcia's disappearance, the Trimble family went to church. Even though she had been a Christian only two years, Mrs. Trimble's faith was almost unbelievable. At her home where great crowds were still walking the street, a reporter asked her a rather unexpected question: "Mrs. Trimble, if Marcia is found alive, and her kidnapper faced you, what would you say?" She hesitated for some minutes, then with a smile, she said, "I would tell him that *God loves him.*" It took undaunted faith on the part of this mother, drenched in heartaches, to make that statement.

LOVE, God's love in the hearts of individuals, is the answer to the world's ills. The only greatness is unselfish love. Love cannot be wasted. It makes no difference where it is bestowed—it always brings in big returns. The coin of God's realm is love.

It is in loving, not just in being loved, the heart is blessed; it is in giving, not seeking gifts, we find our reward, whatever be our longing or our need. Give—so shall your soul be fed, and you indeed shall live. God regards the greatness of the love that prompts the man, such as the Samaritan, rather than the greatness of his achievement.

This is what Jesus was trying to teach the lawyer through the story of the Good Samaritan. And the lawyer saw it at once when he said: "He that sheweth mercy on him" and Jesus said, "Go, and do thou likewise" (Luke 10:37).

Jesus said:

> But I say unto you, Love your enemies, bless them that curse you, and do good to them that hate you, and pray for them which despitefully use you, and persecute you. That ye may be the children of your Father which is in heaven: for he maketh the sun to rise on the evil and the good, and sendeth rain on the just and the unjust (Matt. 5:44-45).

2. They Gave of Themselves

No truly great and generous heart has lacked tenderness and compassion. It has the crown of justice and the glory of God's love as its hallmark. Compassion and mercy are interchangeable virtues. If mercy were not mingled with God's love, this wretched world could not subsist for one hour. That is the message of the Good Samaritan.

Many years ago a dedicated and successful doctor witnessed a demonstration of God's forgiving love. He watched a dying woman in the emergency room of a London hospital to such an extent that it completely changed his future life. He volunteered for medical missions to the poor Eskimos and fishermen on the frozen coasts of Newfoundland and Labrador. Dr. Wilfred Grenfell gave up a lucrative practice and went to minister to those unfortunate people. Through his efforts, hospitals, orphanages, nursing stations, schools, cooperative stores, and industrial centers were set up in the cold, bleak lands of the north Atlantic coast.

One day a call came for a doctor to attend a severely ill man at a small village of less than a dozen families. Grenfell knew it would be a dangerous journey, but when the bearer of the message came ashore and said, "It's the old Englishman; Uncle Solomon, they calls him" the doctor

17

could not resist the opportunity to render the necessary service to the suffering gentleman.

After checking his patients in the hospital and packing what he hoped would be the essential medicines that might be needed, it was nearly midday before they started for the cape where they would land. As soon as they reached their destination, a blck-bearded, bright-faced man of about fifty gave them a hearty greeting. Such evident happiness lit up the man's peculiarly shaped eyes. Dr. Grenfell felt a little more cheerful, even before the man had taken them up to his house. There they found a cup of steaming hot tea prepared. That tea didn't seem a bit less sweet because, "There be nary a drop of milk in this harbor, Doctor, and molasses be scarce, too, 'til the fish be dry."

Everything was clean. The pots and pans and tin cooking utensils shone so brightly from the walls that the flame of the tiny kerosene lamp suggested ten thousand-fold the candle power it possessed.

Three children were playing on the hearth with a younger man, evidently their father. "No, Doctor, they aren't ours exactly," replied the host, in answer to the doctor's question. "But us took Sam as our own when he was born, and his mother lay dead, and he have been with us ever since. Those be his little ones. You remember Kate, his wife?"

The doctor remembered her very well, and the struggle they had trying to save her.

"Skipper John," the doctor said, as soon as the tea was finished, "let's get out and see the old Englishman. He'll be tired of waiting."

"Youse needn't go out, Doctor. He be upstairs in bed."

"Upstairs" was a triangular space. At each end was a tiny window, and the area, windows included, had been divided longitudinally by a single thickness of hand-sawn lumber, up to the cross-beams. There was no lofting, and both windows were open—a cool breeze was blowing through. Cheerfulness was given by the bright white paper which had been pasted over everything. Homemade rugs covered the planed boards.

"Uncle Solomon, it's the doctor," said the host. A trembling old hand came out to meet the doctor's. "Not so well, Uncle Solomon? No pain, I hope."

"No pain, Doctor, thanks to the good Lord and Skipper John," he added. "He took us in, Doctor, when the old lady and I were starving."

When the examination was over, "I found my host's hand on my shoulder," said the doctor. The host said, "You'll be wanting a good hot cup of tea, I know, Doctor. And the wife has made a bit of toast, and a taste of hot berry jam. We are grateful you come, Doctor. But thanks aren't dollars."

"No, Skipper John," was all the doctor could speak. "We doctors, anyhow, find them quite as scarce," answered Grenfell.

"Well, Doctor," the skipper added, "please God if I gets a skin this winter, I'll try and pay you for your visit anyhow. But I hasn't a cent in the world just now. The old couple has taken the little us put by."

"Skipper John, what relation are these people to you?"

"Well, Doctor, no relation 'zactly."

"Do they pay nothing at all?"

"Them has nothing," the skipper replied.

"Why did you take them in?"

"They was homeless, Doctor, and the old lady was already blind."

"How long have they been with you?"

"Just twelve months come Saturday."

"Thanks, Skipper," was all the doctor could say. But the dedicated and unselfish doctor later said, "I just froze in my tracks as I found myself standing with my hat in the presence of this man. I thought then, and I still think, I had received one of the largest fees of all my medical career."

Samaritanship was demonstrated as we will seldom find it in this cruel world. Here was a couple who had nothing of this world's goods except what they could earn from catching fish and a few fur-bearing animals, whose skins they might sell for a pittance, yet they had hearts of gold. Hearts filled with God's love and compassion.

Alfred A. Peterson, an advertising executive in Grand Rapids, Michigan, in his little book, *The Art of Living,* has a chapter on "The Art of Giving." In that chapter he observes:

In gratitude for God's gift of life to us we should share that gift with others. The art of giving encompasses many areas. It is an outgoing, overflowing life.

Emerson said it well: "Rings and jewels are not gifts, but apologies for gifts. The only gift is a portion of thyself." We give of ourselves when we give gifts of the heart; love, kindness, joy, understanding, sympathy, tolerance, forgiveness, compassion. We give of ourselves when we give gifts of the spirit: Prayer, vision, beauty, aspiration, peace, faith.[1]

And Francis of Assisi has given us an even more beautiful
thought in his prayer:

> Lord, make me
> an instrument of thy peace;
> Where there is hatred,
> let me sow love;
> Where there is injury, pardon,
> Where there is doubt, faith;
> Where there is darkness, light
> And where there is sadness, joy.
>
> Divine Master,
> Grant that I may not seek to be consoled,
> as to console.
> To be understood as to understand;
> To be loved as to love;
> For it is in giving that we receive;
> It is in pardoning that we are pardoned;
> It is in dying that we gain eternal life.

3. A More Excellent Way

When God formed the rose, he said, in substance: "Thou shalt flourish and spread thy perfume." When he commanded the sun to emerge from chaos, he said, "Thou shalt enlighten and warm the world." When he gave life to the lark, he enjoined it to soar and sing in the air. Finally, he created man and told him to love his fellowman. And seeing the sun shine, perceiving the rose scattering odors, hearing the lark warble in the air, how can man help loving? As a flower cannot blossom without the sunshine, how can man live without love?

When the apostle Paul became greatly disturbed about what was taking place among his friends in the church at Corinth, he wrote them two letters. In 1 Corinthians 12 he deals at length with the spiritual gifts available to every Christian through the Holy Spirit.

He affirmed: "Now there are diversities of gifts, but the same Spirit." Then he outlined the opportunities of service through the use of these gifts, concluding the chapter with these challenging words: "But covet earnestly the best gifts; and yet I show you a more excellent way." Then follows 1 Corinthians 13, his magnificent chapter on love. Love—the answer to all of the world's problems, God's love in the human heart.

Dr. Henry Drummond, the brilliant English clergyman of many years ago, in his sermon, "The Greatest Thing in the World," gives a splendid outline of this immortal chapter. He breaks it up into three divisions: *Love contrasted* in verses 1-3. In the heart of it we have *Love analysed,* verses 4-7. And toward the end we have *Love defined.*

Then, Dr. Drummond goes even further in his appraisal of Love in a more detailed outline, in which he sets forth the many facets of Love. You will notice he is using very everyday names. They are virtues which we hear about, or should hear about, all the time. They are traits which can be practiced every place in life. By a multitude of small things and ordinary virtues, we can enjoy the blessings as taught by the Good Samaritan.

Patience	"Love suffereth long."
Kindness	"And is kind."
Generosity	"Love envieth not."
Humility	"Love vaunteth not itself, is not puffed up."
Courtesy	"Doth not behave itself unseemly."
Unselfishness	"Seeketh not its own."
Good Temper	"Is not easily provoked."
Guilelessness	"Thinketh no evil."

These make up the supreme gift, the stature of the perfect man. Note that all are in relation to man, in relation to life, in relation to the known today and the near tomorrow, and not to the unknown of eternity. We hear much of love to God—Christ spoke of love to man.

Jesus had built a fire on the shores of the Sea of Galilee, making advance preparation for breakfast with his disciples.

This was the third time he had appeared to them since his resurrection. With breakfast over and knowing that he was soon to leave them, Jesus was concerned about their attitude toward him in the future. Turning to Simon Peter, he asked: "Simon, son of Jonas, lovest thou me more than these? He saith unto him, Yea, Lord; thou knowest that I love thee. He said unto him, Feed my lambs. He saith to him again the second time, Simon, son of Jonas, lovest thou me. Yea, Lord; thou knowest that I love thee. He said unto him, Feed my sheep" (John 21: 15-16).

And even a third time Jesus asked the same question and received the same answer. Yes, Jesus was concerned about the future of his program. It was his hope that his disciples would change the world.

On what did Christ place this hope, this confidence for its accomplishment? Eloquence, learning, faith, earnestness—all are useful, some tremendously important, but the essential thing is love. God's love in the hearts and in the lives of his followers to do his work. Can he trust us? Do we love him? How much? Enough to feed his sheep scattered throughout the world, meeting their various needs? Love is absolutely necessary.

It was a cold December day in 1941. Dr. Howard A. Rusk, a practicing physician in St. Louis, Missouri, had left home early that morning for a good hard horseback ride across the Missouri countryside. Arriving back home, he knew something terrible had happened, because his family looked like ghosts as they greeted him. The radio had just announced that the Japanese had attacked Pearl Harbor. Life was to be drastically changed for him and the rest of America.

Dr. Rusk made plans to close his practice of internal medicine and to volunteer for military service in early 1942. He was assigned to the Army Air Force at Jefferson Barracks just outside St. Louis. He was to lead one of the most complete convalescent programs ever undertaken by the military forces—that of caring for the wounded, who had lost one or more limbs, and others seriously injured in the Pacific War. The program has since been greatly enlarged, with hospitals all over the country, treating other than military personnel.

In his book, *A World to Care For,* Dr. Rusk and his associates explained how they soon learned that they had to treat the whole man—not merely his damaged body, but also his mind and his soul. It became clear that the patient must not only have courage and determination, but also the love of his family and friends. His wife, brothers, sisters, father, mother, and children must all be involved. Whatever the disability, it was never easy for patient or family.

Dr. Rusk cited one particular instance where love was one of the determining helps in healing a patient. The patient was a pilot whose face had been badly mangled and burned. He had been such a handsome man, married only a short time before he was sent overseas. Now, he did not want his wife to see him, at least not until after extensive plastic surgery, which might take weeks before he would be halfway presentable. His wife was insistent that she see him, and one day she came to the hospital and simply would not go away. The doctor tried to reason with her, but she would not budge. Finally, the doctor took her in, though he was full of trepidation.

"Her husband's back was turned; he was looking out the window, shaking with fear. But she walked directly to him, turned him toward her, and kissed him. Then she said, 'John, I love you. You need never worry about me, honey.

I married a man, not a face.' " [1]

After weeks and weeks of hospitalization and extensive skin grafting, John returned to civilian life. All during these experiences, his devoted wife stood by, always lending encouragement. Oh! The power of God's love in the heart of an individual.

It matters not how far one may wander away from God, how deep one may be mired in sin, God is ready to forgive and welcome us back into the fold.

I have mentioned Henry Drummond's message entitled "The Greatest Thing in the World." It is my hope that many of you will have access to a copy. In his closing words, Drummond issues a challenge to all of us: "How many of you will join me in reading this chapter [1 Corinthians 13] once a week for the next three months? A man did that once and said that it changed his whole life. It will do the same for you also."

"Love suffereth long, and is kind, love envieth not, love vaunteth not itself."

Get these ingredients into your life. Then, everything that you do will be eternal.

4. No Greater Love

On February 3, 1943, the troopship *Dorchester* was torpedoed and sunk in the North Atlantic off the coast of Greenland. Four chaplains—a priest, a rabbi, and two Protestant ministers—gave their lifejackets to others and went down with the ship. The fact that the four chaplains' sacrifice was a demonstration in brotherhood makes it even more significant. They showed their concern and love for those in need of help.

Jesus had inaugrated the Lord's Supper in the upper room and was on his way to the garden of Gethsemane. As he and his disciples were walking together, he seemed to have been aware of the events of the upcoming hours and days. This was evidenced by the very intimate conversation he had with his followers as recorded in John 15: 11-13:

"These things have I spoken unto you, that my joy remain with you, and that your joy might be full. This is my commandment, That ye love one another, as I have loved you. Greater love hath no man than this, that a man lay down his life for his friends."

Love of God and love for man are the missing ingredients in the world today. Love is the cure-all medicine for our sin-sick generation. But the word "love" here does not mean fleshly love for the opposite sex, but the divine love

shared by those who know the Lord. Love is the foundation of all that is worthwhile. Love is the biggest thing on
earth. It is the mightiest factor in human experience. And
God's love is so wonderfully deep and strong that it is beyond human understanding.

Love is the foundation of the home; yet, many homes
are being broken up from a lack of genuine love. From the
moment when a man's parents fell in love with each other to
the moment at which his own eyes are reverently closed by
fond and tender hands, life is literally steeped and drenched
and saturated in love. Love of mother and father; the love
of brother and sister; the love of husband and wife; the love
of son and daughter; the love of grandchildren—life should
be one long pilgrimage from love to love. One love escorts
us to another. Amid all the world's chances and changes,
love never fails us.

God was so concerned about lost humanity, and he tried
so hard to demonstrate to the world that there is "no
greater love" than the giving of his Son to die for mankind.

When I think of all these characteristics of love, as outlined in the previous chapter, concrete illustrations from
the life of Jesus come to mind.

Love is the Good Samaritan aiding the man who had
fallen among thieves. Though the victim had no special
claim on him—not nearly as obvious a claim as on the priest
and the Levite who passed by on the other side—the Good
Samaritan interrupted his journey and took care of the man
and made provision for his future care.

Love is what happened one day in Jerusalem. A young
teacher was in the outer court of the Temple. He was
quietly discussing the issues of life and death with a small
group. Suddenly, they were interrupted by some self-

righteous religious leaders who thrust a known prostitute
into the circle and demanded to know what they should do
with her. They knew what the Law said—stone her—and
Jesus knew what the Law said, too. And when his sharp
dealing with the situation had dispelled the crowd and he
was there with the sinful woman, instead of reading her a
severe lesson on how she ought to behave, he told her that
he did not condemn her. He urged her to go and sin no
more. Love is kind.

Love was again demonstrated when the four men brought
a friend "sick of the palsy . . . and when they could not
come nigh unto him for the press, they uncovered the roof
where he was . . . they let down the bed wherein the sick
of the palsy lay. When Jesus saw their faith, he said unto
the sick of the palsy, Son, thy sins be forgiven thee"
(Mark 2:4-5). Again, "So great love."

Love is the father standing at the gateway of his home,
looking down the road and hoping for the return of his
prodigal son from the far country. And when he comes—
foolish boy that he has been—the father goes to meet him
and restores him to the full relationship, refusing to let the
son's admitted foolishness become the basis for a final
judgment. Love is forgiving.

Unthoughtful children are doing the same thing today,
but love will seldom seek revenge or be unkind. "Love is
not easily provoked." An unruly boy, who had given his
parents nothing but trouble, finally ran away from home.
After he was gone, his father wrote him many letters, pleading with him to return home. But the boy stubbornly refused; in fact, he ridiculed his parents for their pleas. Then,
one day he received a telegram saying his father was dead,
and that the rest of the family wanted him to be present

for the funeral. His first thought was to refuse, but he finally decided to go. The least he could do was to pay final respects to the father for whom he had shown so little respect.

The day following the funeral, the family was called together in a special meeting. The father's will was read. With unbelieving ears, the wayward son heard that the father had remembered him, along with the rest of the family. He was to receive the same inheritance as the other children who had not gone astray. This realization broke his heart, and he repented of his misdeeds. But for days he was confounded that his father had loved him in spite of his rebelliousness.

Like the truant's longsuffering father, God loves us to the end of the world. But we must come to God in order to receive our heritage. God's treasures await every one of us. He has named us in his will, making us fellow-heirs with Christ. Our salvation is secure, but we must be willing to accept it. "No greater love" than God's love for his children.

Jesus taught so many helpful lessons through the use of parables—or stories. One of these, unsurpassed in tenderness and beauty, is told only by Luke (7:36-50).

A woman of the street burst through the doorway and fell at Jesus' feet as he was having a meal with a Pharisee named Simon. In a display of passionate repentance, she unleashed a torrential flow of tears. She tenderly dried his feet with her hair and anointed them with expensive ointment. Simon thought within himself that, according to the Pharisee's code, the more righteous one is, the more bound he is to keep the sinner at a distance. Jesus answered his thoughts with the story about two debtors who were forgiven much. Because this woman was forgiven much, she loved much. Forgiveness fills our souls with love. Love expressed in the Lord does not meet a cold restraint. "Wherefore I say unto thee, Her sins, which are many, are forgiven; for she loved much: but to whom little is forgiven, the same loveth little" (Luke 7:47).

God's love for his children is so often demonstrated through little wayside experiences on the part of children. The Christmas season was approaching in December, 1971. A nine-year-old boy in Maryville, Tennessee, adored his widowed mother. He was eager to remember her at Christmas, but he had already used his modest allowance. What could he do?

Getting out his battered, rusty bike, he polished and cleaned it to perfection. Riding downtown to a pawn shop, he told the owner his story. He was going to use the money to buy a Christmas present for his mother. He struck a bargain, leaving the bike behind in hock for eight one-dollar bills. Looking back only once, he commented: "I won't be needing that old bike before next spring, anyway." And out he went to find a suitable gift for his precious mother.

Other than God's love for a lost world, is there any greater love than that of a boy for his widowed mother, and her love for him?

The *Maryville-Alcoa Daily Times,* which related the story of the pawned bike, did not give the name of the boy:

> We are not inviting any warmhearted citizen
> to rush down and offer to get his bike out of
> hock. He will regain it all by himself, which will
> further strengthen his confidence in himself.

5. Because We Love Them

On an outdoor billboard, standing high above a viaduct in our city, the advertisement of a nationally known life insurance company presented a most challenging and thought-provoking picture. The artist portrays several small children playing on the sands of the seashore. In the distance one can see the billowy waves of the ocean. The caption of the advertisement reads, "Because we love them."

Any well-intentioned father who reads this will think of his own children and realize that, in the event of his death or disability, he must provide adequately for his loved ones through life insurance. Every father should show his love for his family by every means possible.

We are not what you would call avid television fans, yet from time to time we find a worthwhile program. This was true when we watched a program entitled "To All My Friends on Shore." It was a realistic and poignant account of a slum family and the father's dream of providing for them a suitable home in a better neighborhood. He had found an old rundown house which he hoped to buy and rebuild. He worked as a scavenger, gathering and selling junk. He saved his money, hiding it in a little tin box which he kept in a kitchen cabinet. The son, an only child, had little opportunity to play with his friends, since he was required to go with the father on his rounds. This brought on tension and unrest in the family, because the mother thought the boy should have more freedom.

Tragedy struck one day as the lad, on a rare occasion, was playing on the playground and collapsed. He was rushed to the hospital. After a lengthy diagnosis, the family was advised that he had leukemia.

This tragedy served to bring the family closer together, and the father realized that in his preoccupation with money, he was tearing the family apart. Not until this illness came was the father able to focus his energies on more important things. From then on he gave himself unreservedly to the welfare of his son. The picture closed with the father renting a motor boat and taking his wife and son for a day's outing at the lake. In this way he tried to demonstrate his love for the son whom he had neglected for a long time and whose days he knew were numbered.

Before Jesus came, God had tried in so many ways to demonstrate his love for mankind. He had shown his power and wisdom in the creation of the world, his wrath in the great flood, his steadfast faithfulness in the covenant which he made with the children of Israel, and his expectations for man when he gave the Ten Commandments. For years and years—by demand, threat, and promise—God had made himself known to his chosen people.

In Jesus, however, God was and is brought into focus for man as never before. In his Son, God shows himself as one who has a personal love for every human being. An awareness of God's love can completely change one's life.

A Chicago business lady was going to work one morning. The bus seemed more crowded than ever before, with each new push and shove. Her exasperation grew until she said to herself: "Is my part-time job worth bucking these crowds every day?" Her self-pity covered many areas: worry over her children's schoolwork, news that two of her husband's co-workers had been discharged for no real reason, and a personality problem in her own office.

Her eyes wandered casually over the advertisements above the heads of the many standees, not really seeing them. Then, her attention caught a tiny sentence someone had scribbled on the bottom of one of the ads: GOD LOVES YOU.

Suddenly it was as if she were seeing with new eyes. She looked at the words again—then at the people around her. She no longer saw them as an irritable, pushing, shoving crowd but as children of God just as she was. At that moment her feelings of irritation and frustration were replaced with a sense of well-being. Certainly she had worries and problems, but the calm assurance of the words, "God Loves You," stayed with her when she left the bus, ready for anything the day might hold. God had spoken in whispers to a troubled soul.

Who can describe the love of God? Who can fathom that little word "so" found in John 3:16 — "God so loved the world that he gave." Poets, musicians, and artists have used every figure of speech to portray that love. But they can give only an imperfect description. The incarnation, the life, and the death of our Lord Jesus Christ represent the love of God seeking the eternal good and salvation of mankind.

The psalmist in Psalm 103 said: "For as the heaven is high above the earth, so great is his mercy toward them that fear him" (v. 11). The love of God is expressed in many ways, but the cross of Christ — in all of its loneliness and

indescribable suffering — will stand out in all eternity as reflecting the love of God beyond measure.

In the same psalm we learn of God's love through
his willingness to forgive: "Who forgiveth all thine
iniquities . . . The Lord is merciful and gracious, slow
to anger, and plenteous in mercy . . . He hath not dealt
with us after our sins; nor rewarded us according to our iniquities" (vv. 8, 10).

For many, many years C. Roy Angell, now deceased was
pastor of the Central Baptist Church, Miami, Florida.
He was an Englishman. Before coming to America, he had
the rare privilege of an interview with Dr. Wilfred Grenfell,
the courageous and intrepid missionary to the fishermen of
cold and bleak Labrador. During this interview Dr. Angell
asked Dr. Grenfell what influenced him to give his life so unreservedly to God. His face grew serious and his tone of voice
almost reverent as he told of this incident:

"Into the hospital where I was a resident physician, a woman terribly burned was brought one night. We all saw immediately that there was not hope for her. We discovered
that her husband came home drunk and threw a paraffin
lamp over her.

"We summoned the police, and when they arrived, they
brought with them the half-sobered husband. The magistrate leaned over the bed and insisted that the patient tell
the police exactly what happened. He tried to impress upon
her the importance of telling the exact truth since she had
only an hour to live. She turned her face from side to side,
avoiding looking at her husband who stood at the foot of
the bed, a miserable creature.

"Finally, her eyes came to rest on his hands and slowly
raised to his face. The look of suffering disappeared from

her face and in its place there came one of tenderness, love, and all the beautiful things that a woman's face can express. She looked back then to the magistrate and said in a quiet, clear voice: 'Sir, it was just an accident.' With a shadow of a smile still on her face, she snuggled down in the pillows and died."

Dr. Grenfell said that he went back to his room and sat for a long time on his bed in meditation. "Finally," he said, "I spoke out loud. That was like God, and God is like that. His love sees through our sins." There is no greater love in the world than God's love for his children.

In late February, 1972, ex-columnist Walter Winchell died of cancer in a Los Angeles hospital. He was a remarkable man in so many respects. The child of a broken home, he was reared by relatives and in foster homes; yet, he reached the top as a radio broadcaster and news columnist. For thirty years most Americans were familiar with his radio opening statement as he shouted, "Good evening, Mr. and Mrs. North and South America, and all the ships at sea. Let's go to press!" Millions listened and other millions read his slangy, three-dot column in the New York *Mirror* and 800 other newspapers.

The last years of Walter Winchell's life were filled with illness and heartaches. His older son took his own life. His wife died two years later; yet, in spite of all these tragedies he worked tirelessly as his strength would permit, raising funds for the Damon Runyon Memorial Cancer Fund. At his private funeral in Phoenix, Arizona, there was a single mourner, his sister, and a Rabbi. Three curiosity seekers stood nearby, and the sister asked them to leave as she knelt by the casket. Later she said: "He died, technically of cancer, but actually of a broken heart." She declined further comment.

Could it be that Walter Winchell's friends had deserted him in the later years of his inactive life? Did he feel that "nobody loved him"? Yes, God loved him because there is "no greater love" than God's love.

On the way to the garden of Gethsemane, Jesus spoke to his disciples and said: "This is my commandment, that ye love one another, as I have loved you. Greater love hath no man than this, that a man lay down his life for his friends. Ye are my friends, if ye do whatsoever I command you" (Luke 15:12-14). He proved his love for all mankind only a few days after this experience. He paid the supreme price for you and for me. Are we grateful for this sacrifice?

6. Love Is Patient

Our real blessings often appear to us in the shape of pains, losses, and disappointments—but let us have patience, and we soon shall see these in their proper figures. There is no road too long to the man who advances deliberately and without undue haste. There is no honor too distant to the man who prepares himself for it with patience. There is no great achievement that is not the result of patient working and waiting. "By their patience and perseverance God's children are truly known from hypocrites and dissemblers," noted Augustine.

Love is patient. This is the normal attitude of love. It is never in a hurry, always calm, ready to do its work when the summons comes. Love often suffers long and is kind.

There is no more beautiful story in biblical literature than that of Jacob and Rachel, as recorded in Genesis 29. For many years Jacob had worked for his uncle, Laban. As compensation for his work, Laban asked Jacob how he could reward him. "And Laban said unto Jacob, Because thou art my brother [in this sense, a term of friendship, since Jacob was Labon's nephew], shouldest thou therefore serve me for nought? tell me, what shall thy wages be? And Laban had two daughters: the name of the elder was Leah, and the name of the younger was Rachel . . . And

Jacob loved Rachel; and said, I will serve thee seven years for Rachel thy younger daughter . . . And Jacob served seven years for Rachel; and they seemed unto him, but a few days, for the love he had to her" (Gen. 29:15-16, 18, 20.

At this point there comes into the picture deceit on the part of Laban, and Jacob did not get Rachel immediately, because she was the younger daughter. The love of Jacob, however, was not to be denied. He was forced to serve seven more years before Rachel became his bride. Patience had received its reward. True love is an ever fixed mark and never wavers no matter how slowly the hands of the clock turn.

Two young people went steady during the last two years in high school. He joined her church, and she gave every evidence of discreet and steady devotion. As graduation approached, the courtship began to quiver and shake. Finally, it broke apart. He wanted to get married immediately—she wanted to go to college. Soon after they broke up, he married another girl.

Love that is not patient, that does not know how to wait and work for its love may not be love at all but only passing whimsy. Whimsy is never an adequate basis for enduring marriage.

And when an enduring marriage is culminated and the first child is born, we really see patience at work on the part of the mother. Look at her when the baby becomes irritable, slow to take its food, restless at night. Calmly she snuggles it in her arms, giving the little one assurance of protection needed to quiet and calm. "Love suffereth long . . . beareth all things." Love is patient.

The writer of James exhorts us to be patient. In James 5

he gives three examples of this beautiful characteristic of a great Christian. "Be patient, therefore brethren, unto the coming of the Lord. Behold the husbandman waiteth for the precious fruit of the earth, and hath long patience for it, until he receive the early and latter rain . . . Take, my brethren, the prophets who have spoken in the name of the Lord, for an example of suffering affliction, and of patience. Behold we count them happy which endure. Ye have heard of the patience of Job, and have seen the end of the Lord; that the Lord is very pitiful, and of tender mercy" (James 5:7-11). In all of this James is referring to the second coming of Christ, but nevertheless it shows how love for Christ can make us patient for his return.

May we think again of the patience of a young mother all during the younger years of her children. In the fall of 1967 and before his death, Ralph McGill, owner and popular newspaper columnist of the *Atlanta Constitution* wrote one of the most intriguing stories entitled "Stamp of Genuine Love." It clearly demonstrates the patience of a young mother who so devotedly loved her little one.

"It is early, yet the fall colors are just beginning to show on the trees, but the most beautiful sight I have ever seen this autumn was a young woman. The place was the crowded waiting room of a large city airport. The name of it is irrelevant.

"The girl was detached from the crowds that came and went, from arriving and departing aircraft. She was oblivious to those who sat around her.

"She was a frail girl. She had been born with a grossly humped back. Her arms, legs and body were thin. They accentuated her back and the bulge of her shoulders.

"Her face, too, was pinched. But it was a happy face,

rich in contentment and love. She had a small baby in her lap. I saw her when she first came in and sat down. She managed the child and a medium-sized wicker-type bag without trouble or show of weariness. She sat down and adjusted the baby in her small lap, reached with her left hand to open the bag, and took from it a brush. She brushed the baby's hair, adjusted its clothing. They rested for a while, the baby quiet and good.

"The young mother looked at her watch. She got up, took the bag and the child, and walked away. Pretty soon she was back. She had somehow, somewhere, warmed a nursing bottle and its content of formula. The baby took the nipple and drank contentedly. The young woman sat there just looking at the baby. The right descriptive word would not come. I could translate it only as an adoration of patience and love.

"Her utter detachment from herself and all of the bustle of coming and going and the laughter and conversation of moving crowds was marked. The child obviously was, for her, utter and complete fulfillment. If her frail body and awkward humped back had any psychological impact, the child had removed it.

"There was no look of suffering on her face or anger at her being misshapen and frail. She was, beyond question, beautiful, quiet, peaceful, patient, kind. Love filled her heart for the little one.

"There were all sorts of faces, reflecting many things. Faces can be telltale of many times. Our society, they say, is a sick one. Name me a well one. But the face of this child-mother was calm and peaceful, evidencing a stamp of genuine love." [1]

7. Scattering Seeds of Kindness

Life is made up, not of great sacrifices or duties, but of little things—in which smiles and kindnesses and small obligations, given habitually, are what win and preserve the heart and secure comfort. Kindness is the golden chain by which society is bound.

We may scatter the seeds of courtesy and kindness around us at so little expense. Some of them will inevitably fall on good ground and grow into benevolence in the minds of others; and all of them will bear fruits of happiness in the bosom from whence they spring. Kindness is the hallmark of the Good Samaritan. Love is always kind.

As you study the days of Jesus and his activities, have you ever observed how much of his life was spent in doing kind things? Study his life with that in view, and you will find that he spent a great proportion of his time simply making people happy, in doing good turns to and for people. God has put in our power the bringing of happiness to those about us, and that is largely to be secured by our being kind to them.

In Longview, Texas, Bob Campbell owns a small grocery store. It is a happy place because Bob makes everyone feel at home. The most unusual thing, however, about this friendly storekeeper is that he has discovered so many ways

42

to translate the Bible passage on "love your neighbor" into action every day of the week.

The child of a poor family is sick; Bob sees that the family gets twenty dollars to buy medicine. A customer's son is severely hurt in an accident. Through the Shrine, the grocer helps get the boy into the Crippled Children's Hospital.

But it's the elderly whom Bob takes special care of—whether customers or family. Every week he takes an elderly customer to town to do her "big" shopping. He helps a man in his seventies with errands and bill paying. His "old folks" love Bob because he makes time to listen to their troubles and treats them with kindness and respect. Someone once wondered what was Bob's secret for getting along with people. Maybe Jean, his wife, had the answer when she said: "Bob gives more than just groceries. He gives love and smiles, never thinking of the lives he has made happy." Said his pastor, "Our town is a better place to live because Bob lives here."

We know personally another man just like Bob Campbell. In the little village of Ridgecrest, North Carolina, Paul Harris, who owns and operates the small grocery store, for over fifty years has been ministering to his neighbors. His store adjoins the post office. If some of the natives fail to come for their mail for several days, Paul knows it and calls them by phone. If anything is needed, regardless of the weather, he is on his way to their house. There is nothing this thoughtful man will not do for a friend. He is kindness in capital letters. Bob Campbell and Paul Harris are genuine Samaritans.

Paul, in writing to the Ephesians, was constantly reminding them of the more Christlike way of life. "And grieve not the holy Spirit of God, whereby ye are sealed unto the day of redemption. Let all bitterness, and wrath, and anger, and clamour, and evil speaking, be put away from you, with all malice: And be ye kind one to another, tenderhearted, forgiving one another, even as God for Christ's sake hath forgiven you" (Eph. 4:30-32). One kind word can completely transform a life.

"Few people know that Madame Ernestine Schuman-Heink, the world renowned opera star, once contemplated suicide. Early in her career her marriage broke up. Sick, hungry, and discouraged, reluctant to bring up her four children in what seemed the very worst of worlds, she decided to kill them and herself under the wheels of a train.

Late one bitterly cold night outside Vienna, she cowered on the tracks with her babies clutched tightly in her arms, waiting for the express to come roaring down on them. Her little daughter called out to her, "Mama, I love you. Please, let's go home."

That childish voice coming out of the darkness brought the singer to her senses. She abandoned her desperate plan and made another try at life. God blessed her. Within a few short years, she was acclaimed as one of the greatest singers of all time.[1]

When we see someone plunged in the depths of despair, a word of kindness may often turn such a person from bitter frustration, even from catastrophe. It should be the aim of every Christian to bring His love and warmth into the cold and desolate lives of those who despair. "Death and life are in the power of the tongue" (Prov. 18:21).

Our country has never known a more popular "after-dinner" speaker and humorist than Will Rogers of the 1920's and 1930's. His famous expression, "I never met a man I didn't like," was his trademark and probably the reason this cowboy humorist never met a man that did not like Will Rogers.

An incident that happened when Rogers was a young cowboy in Oklahoma helps explain it:

"In the winter of 1898, Rogers fell heir to a ranch near Claremore. One day a farmer who lived nearby killed one of Will's steers that had broken down a fence and eaten his young corn. According to ranch custom, the farmer should have informed Will what he had done and why. He did not do so, and when Rogers found out about it, he was fit to be tied. Flaming with wrath, he called a hired hand to accompany him and rode forth to have it out with the farmer.

"During the ride, a blue norther struck, coating the cowboys and their horses with ice. When they arrived at the farmer's cabin, the farmer was not at home. But his wife insisted that the frozen men come in and wait by the fire for his return. Rogers noticed how thin and workworn the woman was. He also noticed five scrawny children peeking at him from behind the various pieces of furniture.

"When the farmer returned, his wife told him how Rogers and his companion had ridden out of the storm. Will started to 'light' into the man; then suddenly he closed his mouth and offered his hand instead. The farmer, unaware of the reason for Will's visit, accepted the proffered hand and invited them to stay for supper. 'You'll have to eat beans,' he apologized. 'The storm has interrupted the butchering of my steer.'

"The two visitors accepted the invitation.

"All during the meal, Rogers' companion kept waiting for Will to say something about the slaughtered steer; but Rogers just continued to laugh and joke with the family, and watch as the children's eyes lighted up every time they mentioned the beef they would eat on the morrow and during the weeks to come.

"The norther was still blowing when supper was finished, so the farmer and his wife insisted that the two men stay for the night. They did.

"The next morning they were sent on their way with a belly full of black coffee and hot beans and biscuits. Still Rogers had not mentioned the reason for his visit. As they rode away, Will's companion began to chide him. 'I thought you were going to lay the sodbuster low about your steer,' he said.

"Will remained silent for a few moments, then replied, 'I intended to, but then I got to thinking. You know, I really didn't lose a steer. I just traded it for a little human happiness. There are millions of steers in the world, but human happiness is kinda scarce.' "[1]

Love is kind and compassionate.

8. Love Is Unselfish

"Love seeketh not her own." The dictionary defines *selfishness* as devoted to oneself. At the same time. it defines *unselfishness* as not putting one's own interest first.

Selfishness can be one of the greatest enemies of a happy home, a contented family. It can destroy friendships. The selfish individual is constantly on the alert to take advantage of others. Why did the two brothers ask Jesus for a seat on each side of him when he came into his kingdom? Selfishness. Why did the little widow give all she had—the two mites? Unselfishness. She was willing to give her all for the good of others.

We seek after this world's goods, but there is no greatness in things. The only greatness is unselfish love. The obvious lesson in Christ's teaching is that there is no happiness in having and getting, but only in giving. And half of the world is on the wrong trail in its pursuit of happiness.

They think it consists in having and getting and being served by others—it actually consists in giving and in serving others. "He that would be great among you," said our Savior, "let him serve. He that would be happy, let him remember that there is but one way—that it is more blessed to give than to receive."

For the Menn family of Appleton, Wisconsin, the journey to Naples, Italy, in December 1969, had begun as an exciting vacation, planned many months in advance. John Menn, a practicing attorney, his wife, Nell, and their two teenage sons, Jonathan and Gregory, had long wanted to see Italy. They spent three delightful days sightseeing in Rome and taking in its many historic places. Then, on the afternoon of December 31, John rented a car and they leisurely drove south to Naples. It was a journey filled with joking and laughter, with little thought that tragedy was ahead.

The parents loved these family holidays. They always felt it was important to participate with their boys because: "They are just with you for so long; then they are off on their own, and the opportunities to be with them are gone forever." Nell used to tell her sons: "I am so glad you came to live with us." Both boys were a delight to her because they were active and multi-gifted.

The parents and boys often had serious talks. One such conversation occurred the previous June after the family had listened to their minister discuss death. "It will happen—to me, to you, to everyone of us. For that reason we should talk about it," he said.

The Menn family did. The boys agreed that an expensive funeral was senseless. They also decided that it was practical and humane for people to designate that their healthy organs be used after their death to aid the living.

On New Year's Day the family toured Naples. On the next day they made the one-hour trip to Pompeii, where their guide gave a lecture on the archeological treasures around them. Then, the group began ambling through the forum of Pompeii. As they passed a small restaurant, Greg turned to his mother and said: "Mom, I have the worst headache I've ever had."

"How long have you had it?"

"About fifteen minutes. I feel sick at my stomach."

John helped his son to the restaurant washroom. Greg vomited, then gasped, "Dad, no . . . oh!" He collapsed in his father's arms.

The restaurant owner drove the family to the Pompeii hospital. Greg was unconscious. Two physicians attributed the collapse to severe food poisoning. John felt relieved until Greg began convulsing. His eyes rolled uncontrollably. His lips took on a bluish hue. His face turned pale and splotchy. . . . "We'll have to get him to the Polyclinic in Naples!" said one of the two doctors.

The family was numb. Their world was broken apart. After extensive examination by other doctors, they had no alternative but to tell the family: We're sorry. The situation is irreversible. Your son has had a massive cerebral hemorrhage." Death came quiety a short time later.

John told the doctors: "It was my son's wish, and it is our wish, that his body be used for medical purposes. His body is young and healthy, and his organs are valuable to people who need them."

The doctors were stunned. They had never experienced such humanitarianism. Arrangements were made immediately for transplants of the different organs.

The story made headlines in all the Rome papers. The Italians were stunned with admiration at such unselfishness. The editor of one leading paper said of John Menn: "You would like to shake his hand, hug him, tell him—if he does not already know it—that all Rome, all Naples, the entire country, are grateful."

It was a sad journey home, but the family was given a sympathetic and gracious welcome. Numerous families and acquaintances left instructions for the use of their organs to help others when death came. In responding to the welcome, John said: "My son, my friend, my boy did much in life, and he did much in death. In a way, he didn't lose his life. He shared it. And he showed others how to share theirs. In death he has earned the gratitude of an entire nation." [1]

All the members of the Mann family were great Christians. When they made the decision six months before Greg's death, all knew what they were doing. They were doing an unselfish act for another person whom they might help—yet, a person who might never thank them. Love is unselfish.

9. Forgiving One Another

Forgiveness is one of the most beautiful words in the English language. God's gracious spirit of forgiveness runs like a golden thread through the Bible. Over and over again God extends to his children unlimited forgiveness. Jesus underscored this truth in answer to Peter's question: "Lord, how oft shall my brother sin against me, and I forgive? till seven times? Jesus saith unto him, I say not unto thee, until seven times, but, Until seventy times seven" (Matt. 18: 21-22). Then, followed the touching illustration of a certain king and his servants, demonstrating compassion and forgiveness for those servants who had done wrong.

The Christian, like his Master, must never stop forgiving. In these experiences related to Jesus, the Master was enlarging the concept of forgiveness far beyond that taught by the religion of his time. He was leaving a new conception concerning man's understanding of his relationship with his fellowman. Jesus was dramatically illustrating the unlimited nature of Christian love, rooted in the nature of God.

Why forgive? Because God forgives us. It is his nature to forgive, and he wants us to be like him. "For if you forgive men their trespasses, your heavenly Father will forgive you; but if you do not forgive men their trespasses, neither will your Father forgive your trespasses" (Matt. 6:14-15).

Jesus was the master storyteller, using parables in many instances. The parable of the Prodigal Son (Luke 15) is the pearl of all parables. There is none other equal to it. It is, as a wise man observed, a "gospel in a gospel." It is vivid, unparalleled, unforgetable. It remains perpetually fresh because it portrays the tragedy in every generation.

And the prodigal has an unbreakable grip on the heart because the prodigal is always with us. In every community some boy or girl is always wandering away, squandering his substance, and often his very life, before he realizes his mistake. His folly and misery are woven into the fabric of the world's life. As long as there are bad boys in the world, this parable will have its mission. As long as men and women have in their heart a hunger which the food of the world cannot satisfy, they will be drawn to the story of the boy who one day came to himself and thought of the bread which he could have in the old home.

The parable is Jesus' picture of God. It is the greatest portrait of our Maker which has ever been produced. Men cannot paint God on canvas. It has often been attempted by some of the world's superlative artists, and every attempt has ended in failure.

When Jesus told this matchless story, the watching Pharisees were sure, as they listened to the first part of the story, that the boy would be lost. The prodigal himself at one time felt irrevocably lost. His friends, his character, his reputation, his inner controls—all were gone. In the courtroom of his soul, he had passed his own sentence of "guilty" on himself. One chance remained. If his old father still loved him, and if he would return in penitence, perhaps his father would take him back as a hired hand. So, turning his back on the swine, he headed for home.

"While he was yet afar off," a forgiving father already had open arms.

That father's pardon could not remove from the boy's life the fearful consequence of his sin. As long as he lived, the scars on his health, his reputation, and his usefulness would be there. But forgiveness could restore the old relationships of mutual confidence and love; and the fight for a new life could be waged, not in a far and hostile country, but at home. God is like that father, taught Jesus.

Those who have the Father's loving and forgiving spirit within them act as God would act. Not what they say, but what they do constitutes the yardstick by which we are to measure them. When, by God's help, we rise to character's mountaintop and act like true sons of God; when we truly understand and forgive, we start a chain reaction of influence that will sweep down the corridors of time, whose final outcome only God can forsee.

Look at Stephen. Beaten to his knees by the savage mob, the blood pouring from the stone wounds in his face, the courageous servant of God dared to pray: "Lay not this sin to their charge." Saul of Tarsus was standing there with folded arms and hatred in his heart, watching Stephen's face. That face reflected the inescapable light of heaven. It was not long afterward that Saul, persecuting all Christians unto death, felt the impact of Stephen's prayer in the blinding light of the Damascus Road. The forgiving God found reflection through Stephen in the heart of Saul, and who would dare estimate the stream of influence down through the ages? Saul became Paul, the most powerful missionary who ever lived.

It takes a great soul to forgive like God. In the space of eighteen months, we have seen a vivid demonstration of forgiveness here in our city, a father and mother whose son lay dying from an automobile wreck—hit by a drunken driver.

We will call him Joe—a sophomore in college. The son of a music director at one of Nashville's largest churches, Joe was a dedicated Christian, active in all phases of his church.

For five days, Joe lay at death's door. Taking turns, his parents never left his bedside. On the fifth day they asked their pastor to arrange a meeting in the chapel of the hospital with the son and parents of the driver. Seated next to the boy, the mother said: "Son, our boy loved sports, especially football—as you do. Our boy never smoked or drank—and I hope you will never do so again. Our son is going to die as a result of this accident, but we will hold no hard feelings against you. We are forgiving you." Joe died a few hours later.

As Jesus hung in agony on the cross, he said: "Father, forgive them; for they know not what they do" (Luke 23:34).

The true forgiving spirit cannot be a halfway matter. It must be all out. Jesus included in his famous prayer: "Forgive us our trespasses as we forgive those who trespass against us." God's forgiving spirit toward us is dependent on our forgiving spirit. They are closely knit. When we forgive, God does! The willingness to forgive, I suppose, is one of the hardest things that most of us face in life. Yet, it is terribly important.

Jimmy Dean, well-known TV star, tells of his own personal experience and how he learned to forgive after years of being unwilling to do so. He admits how he almost despised his father, and it wasn't hard to have that feeling. He was eleven years old when his father deserted the family, leaving a younger brother, Don, and his mother to face a dismal future. He remembers the hurt in his mother's eyes and the numbness in all of their hearts as she tried to explain what they faced in the future if they were to eat and stay alive.

Mrs. Dean opened a one-chair barber shop and cut hair to earn a few cents—picked cotton in the fields around Plainview, Texas, cleaned out chicken houses, milked cows, and did other farm chores. The only clothes the boys had to wear to school were bib overalls. The better-dressed kids taunted them about what they wore. The mother explained to them that wearing overalls was no disgrace. The important thing was what they had in their hearts. Jimmy never heard his mother complain of being poor. Her faith assured them that they would outlast these circumstances.

World War II was at its height. Jimmy had finished the eleventh grade and joined the Air Force. There he met a group of boys who loved music. He and his friends formed a group who would sing here and there for tips. They started doing a good bit of this, and this opened up his musical career. Out of uniform, he became soloist and was making a good living—hitting the "big time" with his own recording of "Big Bad John." Then one day after seventeen years of silence, Jimmy's father called. He wanted money for some wild scheme he had cooked up. Jimmy turned him down flat. These calls continued intermittently, and each time he was refused.

Invited back to Plainview for a concert in the old school's auditorium, Jimmy first declined. Then his mother reminded him of how much he could mean to the community and how proud they were of him. He accepted. On the first row of the audience, he saw his dear old mother in tears of joy. As he recalled the years of poverty and humiliation she had suffered because of his father, all was wiped away. The memory of that occasion came back to him very vividly when his father called again. This time he did not want money. All he wanted was forgiveness, admitting his mistakes. There was a pause in the father's voice. Then he said, "Son, I have cancer. My time is nearly gone."

Jimmy says he looked back over the years and could see the senselessness of holding a grudge and of trying to judge another. "I forgave my father," he said, "and asked to be forgiven, too." A few days later his father was dead.

"I'm sure that last phone call to me helped my father leave this world with a peaceful mind, and I feel it did something for me.

God's forgiving spirit toward us is dependent on our forgiving spirit. They are closely knit. When we forgive, God does. It was hard for Jimmy Dean to forgive, but he did, and was blessed by doing so." [1]

10. Just a Little Silver

One day a very wealthy, but miserly, man came to see his rabbi for counsel. With all of his wealth, he was unhappy. Life meant little to him. The rabbi led him to a window. "Look out there," he said, "and tell me what you see."

"People," answered the rich man.

Next, the rabbi led him to a mirror. "What do you see now?" he asked.

"I see myself," answered the man.

"There is a glass in the window, and there is glass in the mirror. The glass in the mirror is covered with a little silver. No sooner is a little silver added, and you cease to see others and see only yourself."

All of which points up to the profound truth, that material things may easily come between us and the higher purposes of our being. When our blessed Savior answered the query about which is the first and greatest commandment, he not only honored the statute of antiquity, but he vastly enlarged its logical implication: "Thou shalt love the Lord thy God with all thy heart, and with all thy soul, and with all thy mind, and with all thy strength: this is the first commandment. And the second is like, namely this, Thou shalt love thy neighbour as thyself" (Mark 12:30-31).

That left the ancient commandment in its rightful place of preeminence, but it lifted the implied regulation to a level of fresh and vital importance. There is no conflict between these two proposals but rather a divine comradeship—they are part and parcel of the only rightful pattern of life entirely pleasing to our heavenly Father.

How easy it is to have THINGS intrude or impose themselves upon our daily plans of life—to the hurt of life's higher values and purposes. How unconsciously we fall into the habits of the fleshly economy to the tragic limiting of our larger ministries. Yes, even to the neglect of simple kindnesses to friends and neighbors. God has richly blessed us from every standpoint, but privilege and advantages often blind men to the rights and needs of others. You would suppose that those who have much would assume an attitude of forbearance to those who are not so privileged. But in reality the opposite is the truth.

Always remember that, by and large, those who do the work of the world are persons who fear God, love their homes, and are devoted to their country. And yet, there is so much poverty, so much distrust, so much unrest in all walks of life. People at the bottom of the ladder have come to believe that people at the top of the ladder of privileges—whether intellectual, political, social, or economic—have ceased to care. All too many of those who are richly blessed are not troubled enough to ask questions about the heartaches of the world. They can eat their ice cream while their neighbors go hungry. They live in luxury, while in the slums the children of the poor stagger through the streets ill clad and ill fed. The cry of the bruised and broken of the world is never heard: "Is it nothing to you, all of you who pass by on the other side?"

As you see yourself in the mirror, there is another attitude which you may add to the manifold gifts with which God endowed you when he brought you into the world. It is the attitude of stewardship. God has made investments in every life, and through these you may become his instrument for good. The steward of God's grace does not waste his gifts—he uses them to meet the needs of the world. He does not spend them on himself alone—he serves those in need and want.

By that law Jesus lived his life. He was conscious of his privileges and advantages. He had power such as no one ever had, but he did not abuse that power. You hear him declare, "All things are given me by my Father. All power is given unto me in heaven and on earth."

One of the hallmarks of his earthly ministry was that he used his power to minister to others. Knowing that he came from God and would go back to God, he humbled himself, "And took a towel and washed his disciples' feet." There you have the secret of the greatness of Jesus—he never lost his compassion and his sense of service.

Always conscious of his own ability, he cared what happened to the sheep that were lost, to the prodigal who stepped across the threshold of indiscretion. He never lost his compassion for the paralytic who was in constant pain. He carried concern for those souls who were scattered and bruised, for the blind who stumbled through the streets of eternal darkness. He was always doing something for others. He was always seeing people in need, and he used the mighty powers which God had given him for humanity's rebuilding and redemption.

Therein is the test of life. You cannot stand aloof from the heartaches of the world and keep your self-respect.

You cannot separate yourself from the hunger of men and maintain your integrity. You cannot pass by on the other side when you see men struggling, suffering, and dying and expect to receive the commendation of our Lord: "Well done, thou good and faithful servant."

You may have great genius, you may possess superior talents, you may walk through the world with mighty capacities. But if there is no sense of compassion or stewardship in you, if you feel no concern for the misery of the multitudes, then your very abilities and advantages may make a wreck of the world and ruin you. You can do nothing worthwhile in this world without a sense of stewardship. You have to care deeply and show your concern if you are to be a blessing to others.

What is it that turns men's faces toward home at evening? It is not because home provides food and shelter, a convenient place to hang one's hat or rest one's tired body. No, when the world tumbles in, and the supports of life fail, and the lamps go out, men turn their faces toward home because it is the place where people should care and have compassion and feel deep concern for one another. It is the last place to blame and the first place to forgive. It is compassion and concern that gives home the fragrance of heaven.

Big, easygoing Edward Hooker of Muskegon, Michigan, and his wife, Dorothy, were quite shocked one day in early November, 1961. An attorney from New York contacted Mrs. Hooker at the restaurant where she was a cook and gave her the news that the Hookers were the beneficiaries of a relative in Belfast, Ireland, and "somewhere in West Germany." Yes, a substantial estate was theirs. They had been married twenty-one years, and both had worked hard all of their lives. Mr. Hooker, sixty-eight years old at that time, was a retired steel construction "boomer" and power company employee. His wife also worked to augment their income.

After the necessary negotiations and papers were completed, the Hookers made a visit to Ireland to inspect their properties. Soon after their return, Mr. Hooker said: "There have been an awful lot of people in my life who have been very good to me. I'd like to do something for somebody. Now, it looks like I'll be in a position to do it."

He didn't simply look *in* the mirror and see himself. He looked *out* the window and saw people who needed him. He became conscious of his stewardship. He was kind to himself by being kind to others. Happiness is a by-product of an effort to make someone else happy.

Bob Hope, who has entertained kings, presidents, and himself, became quite serious a few years ago when he was awarded an honorary degree from Georgetown University:

"I wish my mother could have been here for this ceremony," he told the graduating class. "She was a realist, and a wise one. I remember her saying, 'Leslie (that's British for Robert), it's not so important that you go to college. What's important is that you get an education.'

"She used to hit me with another bit of old-fashioned wisdom—that every young man received two educations: the first, from his teachers; the second, more personal and important, from himself. But Mom was only a mother, and I didn't pay too much attention.

"A good many years later, a couple of wars later, thousands of moments later, of seeing how much good a few laughs can do for men on the edge of dying for their country, I discovered that the most gratifying kind of education is that which makes a man happy in the knowledge that he's a little bit useful to others.

"For the last twenty years I've been running around the world entertaining fellows your age in jungles, stuck away on sandbars in the oceans, cooped up in nature's iceboxes—and I learned that if you give a little of yourself to others, it will come back in carloads. Today is one of those 'comeback' days."[1]

That was ten years ago, and Bob Hope is still making people happy by his unselfishness. He is aware of his stewardship.

Over forty years ago, Bruce Barton, popular author and newspaper columnist, wrote about the two seas in Palestine. His message still has a challenging message for this generation:

"There are two seas in Palestine. One is fresh, and fish are in it. Splashes of green adorn its banks. Trees spread their branches over it, and stretch out their thirsty roots to sip of its healing waters.

"Along its shores the children play, as children played when He was there. He loved it. He could look across its silver surface when He spoke His parables. And on a rolling plain not far away He fed five thousand people.

"The river Jordan makes this sea with sparkling water from the hills. Men build their houses near to it, and birds their nests; and every kind of life is happier because it is there.

"The river Jordan flows on south into another sea.

"Here is no splash of fish, no fluttering leaf, no song of birds, no children's laughter. Travelers choose another route, unless on urgent business. The air hangs heavy above its water, and neither man nor beast nor fowl will drink.

"What makes this mighty difference in these neighbor seas?

"Not the river Jordan. It empties the same good water into both. Not the soil in which they lie, not the country round about. This is the difference. The Sea of Galilee receives but does not keep the Jordan. For every drop that flows into it another drop flows out.

"The other sea is shrewder, hoarding its income jealously.

"It will not be tempted into any generous impulse. Every drop it gets, it keeps.

"The Sea of Galilee gives and lives. This other sea gives nothing. It is named the Dead Sea."

"There are two seas in Palestine.

"There are two kinds of people in the world."[1]

11. Of More Value Than Many Sparrows

Jesus had summoned his twelve disciples and was sending them out to carry on his ministry. Definite instructions were given about what they were to carry with them and how they were to conduct themselves. For, as he said: "Behold I send you forth as sheep in the midst of wolves; be ye therefore wise as serpents, and harmless as doves" (Matt. 10:16). He further told them of how they would be persecuted and even thrown into prison. But he added "Fear ye not therefore, ye are of more value than many sparrows" (Matt. 10:31).

In the spring months of 1955, the editors of the *Family Weekly Magazine,* a supplement for many Sunday papers, had requested one of their staff writers to prepare a story for the Easter edition. And here is what Miss Patty Johnson wrote:

"You suggested that I write an Easter column, boss, and I've tried. I've thought about the crown and the cross and the lillies.

"But it's no use. My mind keeps returning to Louise.

"I know you never heard of her. That's not remarkable. Hardly anyone knew Louise. We were all too busy. Louise didn't belong. There are a lot of people like that. People for whom the world's doors are locked.

"I guess some outsiders live to a ripe old age that way. Louise couldn't. She swallowed some sleeping pills and a bottle of French perfume and lay in agony for three days, waiting for death to recognize her because life didn't.

"Nobody really loved Louise. She was a stranger in a strange land, with not much to offer except a fragile voice which sang a little and laughed less.

"I met her several times. A lot of us did. For a moment or two, it was fun to try to make languages meet and watch the breathless conversation of her hands.

"But we could all afford to be selective in our charmed circle. Louise was on the outside looking in, her lipstick too bright a badge, her hair too yellow. I thought I might invite her home for dinner sometime, but I never did.

"You know how it is. She wasn't my type. Foreigners are different and you never know what their backgrounds might have been. Besides, I wasn't the only one. Everybody felt the same way. Probably she's no better than she ought to be, they said.

"It's strange. When Louise died, committing even then a sin the world cannot forgive, it was we who bore the stigma, we who found the nails of indifference in our hands and the crown of shame on our heads. We who knew at last Louise died of the love we do not own unless we give it away.

"I'm sorry. I cannot write about Easter bonnets or the glory of the birth of spring. I had to write about Louise. I had to tell you that we no longer cover her grave with flowers of our sorrow and our understanding. Louise needed us in life. In death, we need her.

"There is only her name on the headstone of her grave. But on the stone of our hearts, Louise wrote:

" ' Father, forgive them.' "

What a tragedy! Louise was just a "lonesome little sparrow."no one knew of her value, yet she might have been an uncrowned queen, a literary genius, an artist, a musician. But no one cared for her soul.

Somewhat in contrast there is a story that an official in a Scottish church approached a faithful old pastor and said: "There must be something wrong with your preaching and work, for only one person has been added to the church in a whole year, and he is only a boy."

That very day the discouraged old clergyman was in the church praying when he became conscious of someone behind him. It was the only person he had won to the Lord that year. "Well, Robert," said the old pastor, "what is it?"

"Do you think, sir," inquired the lad, "that if I were willing to work hard for an education, I could become a preacher or perhaps a missionary?" There was a pause, as tears came to the old man's eyes. He set about giving proper encouragement to the one person received in the church that year. At the time, just an unpromising lad, but of "more value than a sparrow."

The lad was Robert Moffat, whose intriguing story is not too well-known to the generation under thirty and even older, but his pioneer work in South Africa blazed the trails to even greater work in the years after he retired because of his age. Yes, even as a lad in his cottage home there had come, all unknown to him, the first beckoning toward the high destiny of his manhood. Years later the shadowy summons to the child became a clear call of duty. Sitting around the fireside with his brothers and sisters while the north wind whistled outside, they listened intently as their dedicated mother read them stories of the daring Moravian missionaries in Greenland and Labrador. God was calling him, Robert Moffat, to the life and work of a missionary, exactly as he had called the men and women of the Moravian church years ago.

None of the great missionary societies in London would accept him, he thought to himself, because he had never been to an academy or college. But this fact did not discourage him. Encouraged by the dear old pastor and others, by the time he reached his eighteenth birthday he left home. He went to Cheshire, England, to work as a gardener. There he came in contact with the Wesleyan Methodists. With his boyish enthusiasm, he threw himself into their work. Larger fields awaited him in Manchester, England, where God led him to Rev. William Roby. To Roby he poured out his burning desire to go wherever God could use him.

One day a message arrived from Dunkinfield that Robert Moffat had been accepted by the London Missionary Society. The great dream of Robert's life had come true.

On September 13, 1861, having said good-bye in the little cottage in Carronshore, Scotland, he left for London. During the weeks before sailing he spent much time visiting the museums where he saw on display the idols worshiped in China, Africa, and the South Seas. He wrote his beloved parents: "Oh, had I a thousand lives and a thousand bodies, I must preach Christ to those ignorant, degraded, despised, yet beloved mortals."

In late October the little party of missionaries embarked on the tedious voyage of nearly ninety days, landing at Cape Town, South Africa. For twenty-two years Robert

Moffat gave untiring witness to the saving power of Christ. The converts were not too many, but a base operation was being established. When Moffat returned to England in March, 1839, no royal potentate or victorious army was ever accorded a more generous welcome. In fact, all over England he was called on to give his testimony.

It was Moffat's influence that constrained another Scotsman to give his life to Africa, a man of "more value than a sparrow." A young doctor was destined to become the peerless missionary of modern times. It was in a boarding house in Aldersgate Street, London, that Robert Moffat became acquainted with David Livingstone. He had finished his theological and medical studies and was waiting for the Opium War to end, so he could go as a medical missionary to China. Meantime, there came that clear-cut, indomitable personality who had braved the wilds of Africa and wrought civilization out of savegery. Everywhere Robert Moffat addressed a public assembly, David Livingstone was there to hear him. In a personal conference Livingstone asked a crucial question, would he do as a missionary to Africa? Yes, came the reply in no uncertain tones, "particularly if you will not go to an old station but will push on into unoccupied fields. In the north," continued Moffat, his eyes blazing with the vividness of recollection, "I have seen in the morning sun the smoke of a thousand villages where no missionary has ever been."

For days Livingstone brooded thoughtfully over the words. "Why wait?" he said. "I will go to Africa." And to Africa he went in 1840. His story of sacrifices, even to death, is immortal. As we visited Westminster Abbey, one of the first things we asked to see was the spot of his interment. With bowed heads we reverently read the inscription, indelibly engraved in marble:

Brought by Faithful Hands
over land and sea
Here rests
DAVID LIVINGSTONE
Missionary,
Traveller,
Philanthropist.
Born March 19, 1813
Died May 1, 1873
At Chitambo's Village, Ulala.

For 30 years his life was
spent in unwearied effort
to evangelize the native races,
to explore the undiscovered
secrets, to abolish the deso-
lating slave trade of

CENTRAL AFRICA

Where with his last words he wrote:

"All I can add to my solitude,
is, may Heaven's richest
blessings come down on everyone,
American, English, or Turk who
will help to heal this open sore
for the world."

And Jesus said unto his disciples as he would have said
to men like Moffat and Livingstone: "Ye are of more value

than many sparrows." And among the untapped generations of youth today there are others like them, if we can
only issue the necessary challenge to win them.

Just as the lad with two little fishes and five barley
loaves may have seemed insignificant to the disciples,
God can take the most inadequate, small life and use it
for his glory.

12. We Need Each Other

Are we humble enough to see how reliant we are on others—how much we truly need each other?

Albert Einstein once said: "Many a day I realize how much my outer and inner life is built upon the labors of my fellowmen, both living and dead, and how earnestly I must exert myself in order to give in return as much as I have received." There are no self-made men these days. How dependent we are upon the efforts and thoughts of those who have preceded us, and those who labor beside us! "Before honour is humility" (Prov. 15:33).

A man was grumbling about the high cost of his television repairs. "Be thankful," said an older, wiser neighbor, "that there is someone able and willing to do the repairs for you."

We all have to make use of the skills, time, and talents of others—the mechanic, the electrician, the farmer, the butcher, and professional people. We should count these as blessings, but do we? Instead, we grumble that they cost us money we would prefer to have in the bank.

Other people and their skills have been given by God for our help and comfort through life. We ourselves have been sent to make the most we can of what talents we possess. We have a duty to ourselves and our families. We also have a duty to others—to society, as a whole. This is how it is in the economy of God. Gratitude to God for a God-given skill is thanksgiving to God.

In your community and mine, we are always dependent on the help of others. At a nearby drugstore, the pharmacist is filling a prescription which the doctor has prescribed for a patient. Around the corner, the auto mechanic is putting new spark plugs in a car from a customer. In a courtroom, an attorney is pleading the case for his client. At the hospital in the maternity ward, a nurse is attending the new-born babies with a loving heart and gentle hands.

At the airport, the pilot and mechanics make the last-minute check on the ship's instruments before heading into the sky and across America or the Atlantic or Pacific. In the classroom at school, the teacher is busy instructing a class of your children. At a busy street intersection where traffic lights have failed, the policeman is directing and untangling a traffic jam so we can move on. Do you get the picture? In our daily lives we need one another—the hands of one another.

It is also like that in the church. We need all the talents of all the members. Some people are more gifted in prayer, some in preaching the Word, a larger number in teaching. Every phase of the church's life is in need of help.

One of the most beautiful stories in religious literature is that of Albert Durer and his picture, *Praying Hands*. As a lad, Albert Durer always wanted to be an artist. The son of a Hungarian goldsmith, Durer was part of a large family. There was little money for him to pursue his profession. Finally, he was allowed to leave home and study with a brilliant artist, but it was understood that he would have to make his own way. During those early days of struggle,

Albert found a friend, a man much older than he, and they decided to live together. The going was rough, and they both became discouraged. Finally, his friend made the suggestion that he would go to work while Albert would continue his studies. Reluctantly, Albert agreed, as the friend urged him not to waste his talents.

The weeks and months passed as the older man worked in a restaurant, washing dishes, scrubbing floors, and doing odd jobs. His hours were long, and the work, menial and hard. But he did it cheerfully because he was helping his young friend, looking forward to the time when he, too, might return to his brush and paints.

At last the day arrived when young Albert came home, bringing the money he had received from a wood carving. It was sufficient to buy food and pay the rent for many months ahead. "Now," he said, "the time has come for me to be the breadwinner, and you, my friend, shall return to your paints and brushes." So, his friend left his dishwashing and scrubbing and returned to his life-long ambition to become an artist—but he was in for a shock. The hard work had stiffened his muscles, enlarged his joints, and twisted his fingers so that they would no longer hold the brush with mastery and skill. Sadly, he realized that his art would forever have to be sacrificed.

When young Albert learned what had happened to his friend, he was filled with overwhelming sorrow. He could not give back his skill, but he resolved never to neglect his friend. One day he returned to his room unexpectedly and heard the voice of his friend in prayer. He entered softly, seeing the work-worn hands folded reverently in prayer. Overwhelmed, a great thought came to Durer.

He said to himself, "I can never give back the lost skill

of those hands but I can show the world the feeling of love and gratitude which is in my heart for his noble deeds in our time of need. I will paint his hands as they are now, folded in prayer, and the world will know my appreciation for a noble and unselfish character. It may be that when people look at the picture, they will remember with love and devotion all hands that toil for others and, like me, express in some way their appreciation for such unselfish and beautiful service." Oh! how much we owe to other people in many fields of service. Oh! how we need each other.

And there are people who do care and who want to help.

It was a hot summer day in the beginning of summer when the old man's next-door neighbor found him digging six holes in the ground. "What are you doing, John?" he inquired.

"Planting peach trees," the eighty-year-old gentleman replied.

"Do you expect to eat peaches from those trees," the neighbor teased.

"Nope. At my age, I know I won't," the old man replied. "But all my life I have enjoyed peaches—but never from a tree I planted MYSELF. I wouldn't have had any peaches if other men hadn't done what I am now doing. I'm just trying to pay the other fellows who planted trees for me."

We who live with the advantages of Christianity owe a huge debt to those who have gone before us, and who have suffered much to provide the blessings of Christ which we now enjoy. Each of us, as Christians, can repay that debt in some measure by doing now what they did in their day— by giving of our best to insure those same blessings for generations to come. Then with Paul we can testify: "I have planted, Apollos watered, but God gave the increase" (1 Cor. 3:6).

13. Those Other Hands

A successful business executive had been invited to bring the commencement address to the senior class in a medium-sized midwestern city. On arrival he had occasion to become acquainted with the most prominent businessman in the city, possibly the chairman of the school board. During their visit together, the local man—when being commended for his success—said "Yes, sir. Hard work done it, hard work and sticking to it." Rather crude language, we will admit—but he was being honest as he saw success from his point of view.

Using this fact as a strong point in his address, the speaker admonished the school graduates to do likewise as they entered college and later assumed many of life's responsibilities. People in the community seemed to accept the statement at face value, but one old resident could not help asking the local businessman: "Didn't that $14,000 you inherited from your old man help you none?"

He was right. For years the man's father had toiled to care for his family and to accumulate a modest sum as an inheritance. Let us recognize "other hands" in our success and in our accomplishments. We may not have an inheritance of money, but it is even better when we inherit a good name, good character, good health, or good discipline.

No man is an island. The truly successful person attributes his achievements to the helpfulness of friends and family.

As a pastor approached the home where death had claimed the father, ninety-two years of age, a man stepped from a cab. They both reached the house about the same time. Introductions were in order, and the local minister learned that the visitor had left his business more than 500 miles away and had come to comfort the family in their loss.

"What led you to come so far under the circumstances of this visit?" inquired the local minister. The man replied: "This man threw a generous light in my pathway many years ago. I shall always be indebted to him. I would have come any distance in this hour to lend a little comfort to the family. I have become quite successful in my business, but I try never to forget a friend."

After the interview of Jesus with the woman at the well, his disciples seemed to question his visit with a Samaritan. And Jesus answered them: "And herein is that saying true, One soweth and another reapeth. I sent you to reap whereon ye bestowed no labour; other men laboured, and ye are entering into their labours" (John 4:37-38). He was referring to the saints of old—Moses, Elijah, Joshua, and David—and the whole roll call of faithful men and women, as recorded in Hebrews 11. And how indebted we should be to the "other hands" of those faithful servants of God.

Today, we are too often reminded of the sacrifices which were made by thousands of people in the uncalled-for war in Vietnam. World War I and World War II were fought to help preserve American democracy from the ravages of Nazism and totalitarianism like Communism. Our soldiers and sailors responded to the call to duty, led by men of high and noble ideals, remembering the sacrifices of our forefathers in delivering America to freedom from British kings. Yes, "other men have laboured" that we might enjoy freedom of religion, freedom of speech, and freedom of the press.

On a Civil War memorial in Arlington National Cemetery, where annually on Veterans' Day the leaders of our nation gather to honor our veterans, there is engraved in stone these memorable words:

> Not for fame or reward
> Not for a place or rank
> Nor lured by ambition
> But in simple obedience to duty
> As they understood it
> These men suffered all
> Sacrificed all
> Dared all
> And died.

These words of praise are not just reserved for the dead, but for the living as well—who dared all then, as they do today, in the eternal search for peace with honor.

Never were truer words written than the apostle Paul's in Romans 14:7 and again in 1 Corinthians 3:9: "None of us liveth to himself, and no man dieth to himself." "For we are labourers together with God; ye are God's husbandry, ye are God's building."

A controversy had arisen among the Romans about what constitutes conduct under certain situations, and it was about to threaten the harmony of the first-century community. Paul made it clear that Christians must work together,

that they are dependent on each other. Many observers
would disagree, however. They think they can live to
themselves and that what they choose to do is nobody's
business.

But life is not so simple that a person can do with it
"what he wants to" without concern for its effect on
others. Daniel Boone, living in a log cabin in the woods,
said to his wife in disgust—because other people were beginning to cross the Appalachians and settle in his area—
"Come on, old woman. Let's pack up and move on.
They're beginning to crowd us!" But the world no longer
provides room to move on. We must live together and try
to be at peace with each other. Our mutual dependence
compels us to face the fact that we are dependent on each
other and those "other hands."

At every turn we need one another's help. From the
simple matter of putting the breakfast on the table, all the
way to highly complex medical procedures which daily
save thousands of lives, we are dependent upon one another
all over the world.

Look at one small area of our mutual dependence: an
American child who steps on a rusty nail may owe his life
to a Japanese scientist, Kitasato, who isolated the bacillus
of tetanus. A Russian child saved by a blood transfusion
is indebted to Landsteiner, an Austrian. A German child
is shielded from typhoid fever with the help of a Russian,
Metchnikoff. An American missionary in Africa is pro-
tected from malaria because of experiments of an Italian,
Grassi, while a soldier wounded in battle escapes death
from surgical infection, because of the work of a French-
man, Pasteur, and a German named Koch.

None of us lives to himself. We must sound this note

all across America. Selfish living is deadly. We cannot afford the luxury of living just for ourselves. Every problem of church, community, or nation must at last be submitted to the court of mutual responsibility. We are involved with each other. As John Donne, sixteenth-century English poet-parson, put it: "No man is an island, entire of himself; every man is a place of one continent, a part of the main; if a clod be washed away by the sea, Europe is the less. . . . Any man's death diminishes me, because I am involved in mankind."

It happened some years ago in Stockholm. A woman, hurrying toward a tramcar, stumbled in front of the moving car and was caught underneath it. Immediately someone sent for a crane in order to lift the heavy car and release her.

In the meantime a crowd of people gathered. A man pushed his way toward the crowd, crawled underneath the car, and said to the woman: "Take my hand." She took his hand and felt the nearness and warmth of this stranger. This was sufficient to calm her and to prevent her from going into shock.

When the crane arrived and the woman was released, she exclaimed: "I never thought an outstretched hand could mean so much."

God has stretched out his hand to help us. Being helped by him, we should be able to help others take hold of his outstretched hands. And all we need is a hand—and the willingness to stretch it out. Christians are called to do Christ's work of love on earth.

14. What Can I Do?

There is no more beautiful scene in the family circle than that of a child as he kneels at his mother's knee, or by his bedside, and has his evening prayer. One night a little boy surprised his mother by concluding his prayer for all the family and himself with: "And God, what can I do for you?" This simple prayer from an innocent child should be a challenge to all of us.

For many years George Matthew Adams blessed his readers through his syndicated column of essays. One day he received a letter that read like this: "I would like to do so many things, but I am so little. I want to help, but I don't know the way." Mr. Adams responded through his column by reminding his friend that it isn't the bigness of things or of people that counts. It's the way in which the best use of one's ability fits into the scheme of the world.

There is so much to do. That's about the only discouraging fact about one's brief life on earth. There seems to be so little time to do so many things. But if we will try to do all that we are able to do in the time allotted to us, we need not worry. You can be quite big, right where you are.

The piccolo is the smallest instrument played in a band— but just let its player get off on the wrong key and watch the expression of the bandmaster's face. On a bronze plaque just outside the entrance to the Vanderbilt University Athletic Office, I found these words by the well-known sports writer, Grantland Rice, a 1901 graduate:

> For when the one Great Scorer comes
> To mark against your name,
> He writes, not that you won or lost,
> But how you played the game.

Do many little things, and you will be growing into bigger things. That's how the biggest things come about. Infinite pains, great patience, long and difficult work—these are the roads over which genius walks.

There are no unimportant jobs in the service of the Master. It is quite easy for the janitor to feel that he is insignificant, since he is not the pastor of the church. Yet, God needs both pastors and janitors. One of our local Baptist churches employed a new custodian or janitor. He was not a Christian but soon was converted, and you will never come in contact with such a transformed person. Today the church is his castle. Finishing his duties after Sunday School, he slips into the morning worship service, hungry for the gospel message. He never misses any of the services throughout the week. His task may be considered humble, but he finds great satisfaction in doing what he can for the Savior he has come to love.

All of us have to fight against that subtle feeling which repeatedly comes to us—which seems to challenge us to show reason why we should keep going, why we should do the right and noble thing, why we should see dignity and greatness in doing our work. We are tempted to become discouraged. Why shouldn't we let things drift and find their own way, shape their own ends? The main reason is that all initiative is lost the minute we lower the golden goal and desire for usefulness that is the heart of the soul.

Many sages have remarked that happiness is a state of mind. I like to think of happiness as a state of action, of earnest striving for something worthwhile involving others. When you secure happiness of this variety, there comes to you an overwhelming sense of usefulness which lifts you up, drives you on, nourishes your bodily and spiritual life. Those who give their total efforts to the mere making of money or advancing their own fame miss what life is all about.

This approach to what you can really make of your life is so dramatically illustrated in contrast by the story about the rich young ruler. When he ran to Jesus and asked him: "Good Master, what good thing shall I do, that I may have eternal life?" he revealed many things. He revealed a heart hunger that wealth, position, and youth has not satisfied— the insufficiency of a moral life as a basis for salvation, a seeking attitude with reference to salvation. He was facing one of life's greatest decisions.

The young man was stunned when Jesus said: "If thou wilt be perfect, go and sell that thou hast, and give to the poor, and thou shalt have treasure in heaven: and come follow me" (Matt. 19:21). Jesus had discerned the young man's difficulty, namely, the cancer of covetousness was eating his heart away. Jesus prescribed a drastic operation of complete renunciation and undivided devotion to Christ. But, no, this was too high a price to pay. His decision was disappointing to Jesus. It showed that he lacked the correct sense of values and unwillingness to pay the price of discipleship. It is disappointing when a person comes so near to the kingdom but turns away to face life, death, and eternity without God and without hope.

The Lord recorded the story of the young man that others might read of this man's blunder and profit thereby. We who read and hear the gospel proclaimed are urged to heed the lesson taught and accept Christ at whatever cost.

What can I do? One of our first responses is, as Paul and Silas said to the keeper of the prison, "Believe on the Lord Jesus Christ and thou shalt be saved, and thy house" (Acts 16:31).

Evangelistic opportunities are always present among those we contact in the daily walks of life. At home, in the office and shop, in the marketplaces of our cities, there is always the chance to speak a good word for Christ.

What can I do during special revival services in my church? I can be praying. The only circumstance that can keep me from it is carelessness. In prayer fellowship, I will be close to God's heart of love and will seek the salvation of others.

I can be talking! We talk every day, so why not let our talk be inviting people to know the Lord Jesus Christ as we know him? I will talk up the revival, and not down.

I can be true! In the midst of wrong, I will hold to the right. In the midst of crookedness, by God's grace I will walk uprightly. There can be a clear ring in my life that will be a credit to my Lord.

I can be faithful! I can be found in my place. I can be counted on. I can give full proof of my own faith and love for my Lord by my prayerful presence. When the roll is called for service, I will be there.

What can I do? There is nothing more rewarding than

the role of a Christian teacher, whether in our Sunday Schools or in our secular schools. Horace Mann, one of the great educational leaders, observed many years ago that "education is our only political safety. That a teacher who is attempting to teach without inspiring the pupil with a desire to learn is hammering on cold iron." None can teach admirably if not loving his task.

If I may speak personally, some of the most satisfying and rewarding years of my life were spent in teaching classes of young men. These years were followed by fourteen years as superintendent of the Intermediates (now Youth) of our church. It was not always easy, but the results were far more than I could have dreamed of. I was forced to do extensive Bible study and research so I could share its blessings with those youngsters and others. I learned that when we are helpful and encouraging to others, the blessings are manifold. That overwhelming sense of usefulness makes life more worthwhile. It is like gathering flowers of many colors to add a touch of beauty to the home.

Whistling cheerfully, a boy was hoeing corn one hot summer day when a passerby stopped and said: "My lad, I'm curious to know how you can hoe corn on a hot day like this and whistle while you work."

"Well, sir," the boy replied, "I don't know, unless it is I feel I am doing something that even God couldn't do if I wasn't here to help him."

To bring salvation to all men, God willed to work through us. He has given each of us a part to play. His plan for changing the world includes our willing cooperation. He forces nothing upon us. He asks us to go in his name to all men, as far as we can reach. Without him, of course, we can do nothing.

For many years Mrs. Annie A. Ziedman worked with her husband in a Jewish rescue mission in Toronto, Canada. Out of her experiences she wrote this bit of verse:

> I wiped a tear from off my brother's face,
> And suddenly God spoke, and gently similed,
> "Thank you, my child.
> Some day I'll wipe the tears from every face.
> Till then, you take my place."
> Now since that day, these hands of mine are His,
> Who formed the world, the stars, and all that is.
> My hands, so frail and weak, O wonder grand!
> Are deputy for God's almighty hand.

What can I do? O wonder grand! I can be a witness for God every day of my life. "And whatsoever ye do, do it heartily, as unto the Lord, and not unto men; knowing that of the Lord ye shall receive the reward of the inheritance: for ye serve the Lord Christ" (Col. 3:23-24).

15. Losing Oneself in Service

Few men of the twentieth century have demonstrated the true spirit of the Good Samaritan as much as that humanitarian, Dr. Albert Schweitzer.

One day a group of young people asked him to give them a motto for life. "It is SERVICE. Let this word accompany you throughout your life. Let it be before you as you seek your way and your duty in the world. May it ever be recalled to your mind if you are ever tempted to forget it or set it aside.

"It will not always be a comfortable companion, but it will always be a faithful one. And it will be able to hand you happiness, no matter what the experiences of your lives are. Never have this word on your lips, but keep it in your hearts. And may it be a confidant that will teach you, not only to do good, but to do it simply and humbly.

"I don't know what your destiny will be, but one thing I know; the only ones among you who will be really happy are those who have sought to serve."[1]

The bold, one-inch headlines across the front page of our morning paper, NURSE HOLT DIED AS SHE LIVED . . . HELPING OTHERS, were not only shocking but also tragic. She was the victim of a reckless driver.

Miss Betty Anne Holt was anticipating a happy evening

with a good friend. They had just entered a restaurant on one of the highways leading into our city when someone rushed in and said that an elderly couple had been struck by a speeding car as they walked along the highway only one block from their home. No one seemed to respond to the news, so Betty told her escort: "I guess I ought to go out there and try to help."

She examined the lady who was lying on the side of the road and realized that she was already dead. Then she went to the man, who was lying in the middle of the road, and she tried to stop his bleeding. She asked her friend to get something to cover him, and thus avoid his further shock. But he never made it. Another motorist failed to respond to volunteers with flashlights and waving arms and ran over the man and the nurse. She was rushed to the hospital, but she died within two hours.

When she left her table in the restaurant, Betty Anne never once thought she would have to give her life in an effort to help someone else, but as a registered nurse she was a dedicated and unselfish individual. An ardent lover of her home and family, she had helped to educate her three younger sisters and a brother and paid off the mortgage on her parents' home. Helping the sick in Nashville hospitals and elsewhere was only a part of the way she lost herself in service and concern for others.

Jesus was the master teacher when it came to demonstrating concern for others. In his Sermon on the Mount, he gave us many lessons of how a Christian should live and witness to others. He said: "Ye are the salt of the earth . . . ye are the light of the world" (Matt. 5:13-14). He was indicating the high vocation of those who possess the Christlike personality. What did he mean when he declared to the group, "Ye are the salt of the earth?"

Salt has many characteristics, many functions. It seasons—that is the way most housewives use it. But it is also a preservative, a preventative. It is the open enemy of decay, the foe of impurity. It purifies and sweetens and keeps sound all with which it comes in contact. When it is applied to another substance, it literally enters into the new substance and loses itself.

Christians are like that, Jesus teaches. When we, as followers of Christ, are like salt to the earth, we function as salt does. We relate to others in such a way that we really lose ourselves in the process of helping them become their real selves.

Without the presence of those who are Christlike, civilization does not climb upward but goes downward. Society does not become purer, but it tends to moral rottenness and decay. The presence of a Christlike character in the world is an absolute essential if the world is to keep from disintegration. The same is true of individuals. A Christlike man or woman can change the complexion of his neighborhood and community.

On the roster of names distinguished for humanitarian enterprise, that of young Tom Dooley still shines brightly. Even though he died of a malignancy in January, 1961, his life was an illustrious example and notable for its reminder that, in an age of turmoil and jangling conflict of materialism there are still noble ideals to inspire, share, and serve. He was a young man with a dream, a magnificent dream of helping people in desperate need, of losing himself in service to others.

That was Tom Dooley's goal. Touched by the misery he saw in the Orient while on wartime duty in the Navy, he determined to help provide medical facilities that would bring at least some ray of hope into an area full of tragic want. In 1954, his ship aided in the evacuation of refugees from Communist Vietnam. Seeing and feeling the plight of disease-wracked inhabitants of the area made up Dooley's mind. He had no money, but he had a fighting heart, boundless energy, and a burning desire.

With three of his Navy buddies, he set up a small hospital in Laos. Later they gave it to the Laotian government. For the next five years, despite his malignancy, he drove himself unmercifully, raising funds and supplies for other hospitals. Speaking in our city, he said: "We are not put on this earth . . . to vegetate, but to seek a channel where we can be of service to others." The world is a better place for Dr. Tom Dooley's having lived. He found his sense of purpose, and he fulfilled his mission to the end, always doing the will of God, always following the spirit of the Good Samaritan.

When you stand before God to render your final report, he will not ask you: how popular you were during life, how many parties you went to, how well dressed you were, how much fun you had for yourself, how many clubs you belonged to, how big a bank account you had. *But he will ask you what you did for others.*

If in Christ, you have helped the less fortunate to get food, clothing, and adequate shelter and if you have brought to the afflicted the loving care they need, then you will hear the Master's thrilling invitation: "Come, ye blessed of my Father, inherit the kingdom prepared for you from the foundation of the world" (Matt. 25:34).

Why this extraordinary reward? Listen again to Christ's answer: "For I was an hungered, and ye gave me meat; I was thirsty, and ye gave me drink, I was a stranger, and ye took me in; naked and ye clothed me. I was sick and ye visited me. I was in prison, and ye came unto me" (Matt. 25: 35-36).

But if you thought only of yourself and better food, clothing, and housing for yourself, you will hear the most awful condemnation imaginable: "Depart from me, ye cursed, into everlasting fire, prepared for the devil and his angels" (Matt. 25:41).

Though the lesson from "salt" is difficult to put into practice, there are those to whom we have a definite responsibility. We must lose ourselves in the interest of our children, our families as a whole, and our neighbors. "If any man will come after me, let him deny himself, and take up his cross, and follow me. For whosoever will save his life shall lose it; and whosoever will lose his life for my sake shall find it" (Matt. 16:24-25).

As salt must give itself, so must we—in the interest of others.

16. Life's Detours

Since the beginning of the automobile age and cross-country travel over the nation's highways, one can seldom journey any great distance without running into detours. This has also been true in towns and cities. We grumble impatiently and pause to glare at the barrier in the road as if it were to blame. The detour is usually rough and dusty and often provokingly lengthens our trip. Yet, the route change is unavoidable, and if we are only patient, it soon brings us back to the main highway.

Life's highway likewise has detours. Perhaps sickness intervenes, or we miss a goal we have set our hearts on. Yet, if we follow God's directions, we will overcome the difficulty, however insurmountable it may seem. Though we have been forced to exchange the smooth road for a rough one where we inch forward only with bump and jolt, the main highway may show up at the next turn. For us, as for Christ, "the way of the cross leads home." The detours of sickness or accident may even lead to death, but along the way God is always our guide and protector. Amazing experiences often occur along life's detours, resulting in blessings for the individual and for the world.

Lives lived in unclouded sunlight are not always the most beautiful, just as trips without detours are not always the most rewarding. Even a life filled with sorrow and struggle can inspire many. What blessings stem from such lives! Too much sunshine can turn a life into a desert.

There is no more touching story in biblical literature than that of Joseph. Nearly a third of the book of Genesis is devoted to the life and problems of this servant of God (Gen. 37-50). And all through this record we read over and over again: "And God was with Joseph." Why? He seems to have been one of God's chosen servants, yet all along his journey, he was constantly running into detours.

Joseph was a spoiled boy, the pet of his father. He was arrogant, dreamy, and overbearing. His haughtiness made his brothers furious to the extent that they sold him as a slave into Egypt. His famous coat of many colors was taken back home to his old father, who was told that Joseph was dead. This was the lad's first detour. He was taken from his home, family, and friends.

Later he was sold as a slave to the house of Potiphar, "an officer of Pharaoh, captain of the guard, and an Egyptian." He soon became most popular, finding grace in the sight of Potiphar. But, adversity lay ahead for this noble young man. A second detour awaited him. An attempt was made by Potiphar's wife to entice him to commit adultery. Joseph refused. A second time she endeavored to entice him, and again he refused. Through her evil plotting, she pursuaded Potiphar to punish an innocent man. Joseph was sent to prison.

Again, God was with Joseph. Prison did not break him; it gave him the strength of iron. He proved himself by becoming a comforter to his chained companions, interpreting their dreams, leading to further favor with Pharaoh. It was a lucky day when he was let out of prison and asked to interpret his master's dream, and a better day still when his interpretations proved true, leading to still another detour. Beloved by Pharaoh, a lowly Hebrew slave boy was made prime minister of all Egypt.

The rest of the story is familiar, yet there is no more beautiful scene in all biblical literature than when his brothers, driven by the whips of famine, stood before him. His forgiveness of the brothers who had treated him so shamefully when he was much younger was like Christ's.

> Then Joseph could not refrain himself before all them that stood by him; and he cried, Cause every man to go out from me. And there stood no man with him, while Joseph made himself known unto his brethren. And he wept aloud . . . and Joseph said unto his brethren, I am Joseph; doth my father still live? And his brethren could not answer him; for they were troubled at his presence. And Joseph said unto his brethren, Come near. And he said, I am Joseph your brother, whom ye sold into Egypt. Now therefore, be not grieved, nor angry with yourselves, that ye sold me hither; for God did send me before you to preserve life . . . so now it was not you that sent me hither, but God (Gen. 45:18).

Yes, Joseph was a brilliant, benevolent ruler. Success failed to spoil him, despite his many detours. He proved to us that a good man, wherever he may go, cannot put himself beyond God's care. "The eternal God is thy refuge, and underneath are the everlasting arms" (Deut. 33:27).

Detours, caused by illness, have so many times provided a rich blessing to the individual, and through them to the world. Some of the world's most stirring literature has come from the minds and hearts of men who, through adversity, proved themselves stalwarts in their chosen professions.

If you allow your imagination to slip back almost 300 years, you may see on a warm sunny day a man clad in a grey coat of coarse cloth. He is sitting outside his house in Artillery Walk, Bunhill Fields, London. The rays of the sun bring him warmth, but no light. The passing episodes of the street provoke from him no comment. He cannot see them. He belongs to the pathetic fellowship of the blind. Nor is blindness his only affliction. He suffers the tortures of gout. His hands are knotted with arthritis. His feet are so painful that he is often unable to walk. What a picture of helplessness! What a shut-in kind of life the man must live! At an age when he ought to be at the summit of his poers, he is "cribbed, cabined, and confined" by these dire afflictions.

Who is he?

He is John Milton. He has not always been blind. In his youth he distinguished himself at Cambridge as a scholar. In his early manhood he traveled extensively all over Europe. Later, he became Latin secretary to the Council of State, under Oliver Cromwell. And now he sits there at his front door, a blind and striken man. What an inglorious end to so glorious a beginning. What a depressing evening to a morning so bright!

But Milton did not permit his afflictions, this detour of life, to terminate his usefulness. Today, all the world knows how nobly Milton "served" while he could only stand and wait as he traveled one of life's detours. In his blindness and manifold afflictions, he produced his *Paradise Lost* and his *Paradise Regained*, together with an abundance of other literature which has brought three centuries of enrichment to mankind. From a life so shut in, he found a way of escape. Amid circumstances so limiting, he discovered a path of eminent usefulness. When his outer vision failed, the inner light burned more brightly, and what he beheld he dictated to others so it might be recorded for the benefit of future generations. His weakness became a vehicle of power. To every afflicted, shut-in life, the triumphant spirit of John Milton brings this abiding word of comfort and hope. "The Lord is my light and my salvation; whom shall I fear? The Lord is the strength of my life; of whom shall I be afraid?" (Ps. 27:1). "God is our refuge and strength, a very present help in trouble" (Ps. 46:1).

Few Christians, if any, of the first century faced such a dramatic detour in their life plans as did the apostle Paul. His story is well known to every dedicated Christian of today, but to refresh one's memory we quote briefly the story of his conversion.

> And Saul, yet breathing out threatenings and slaughter against the disciples of the Lord, went unto the high priest, and desired of him letters to Damascus to the synagogues, that if he found any of this way, whether they were men or women, he might bring them bound unto Jerusalem. And as he journeyed, he came near Damascus; and suddenly there shone round about him a light from heaven; and he fell to the earth, and heard a voice saying unto him, Saul, Saul, why persecutest thou me? And he said, Who art thou, Lord? And the Lord said, I am Jesus whom thou persecutest; it is hard for thee to kick against the pricks. And he trembling and astonished said, Lord, what wilt thou have

me to do? And the Lord said unto him, Arise, and go unto the city, and it shall be told thee what thou must do (Acts 9:16).

Paul pulled in the poles of his ancient world and bound them to the cross. He threw open to the Gentiles the doors of the Christian church and bade them come in. Along the way the grand old missionary was whipped, stoned, starved, frozen, shipwrecked, half drowned, and finally beheaded. None of these things could clip his wings. He knew his life was safe. His union was with Christ, his eternal security.

Self-sacrifice was his life's law. Calvary was his passion. Paul taught principles rather than rules. He was as courageous as he was faithful, as indifferent to criticism as he was stubborn for righteousness. He was one of truth's dominant heroes, Christianity's noblest martyrs, the pivotol portrait in the galley of the soldiers of the cross. His faith never flinched.

In writing to the Romans he voiced over and over his abounding faith in Christ.

Who shall separate us from the love of Christ? shall tribulation, or distress, or persecution, or famine, or nakedness, or peril, or sword . . . Nay, in all these things we are more than conquerors through him that loved us. For I am persuaded, that neither death, nor life, nor angels, nor principalities, nor powers, nor things present, nor things to come; nor height, nor depth, nor any other creature, shall be able to separate us from the love of God, which is in Christ Jesus, our Lord (Rom. 8:35-39).

There is no greater love!

17. What If God Had Said "No"?

As the graduates of our colleges and universities reach commencement after their years of study and preparation, it is always a time of happiness and rejoicing. Yet, there is also a bit of sadness because friends must separate and go out to work in their chosen fields of service. There is always much activity around the college campuses, as alumni, friends, and members of the students' families come for the graduating exercises.

The homes of many college professors are often the gathering places for students during their school days, and for friends at commencement time. It was to one of these homes at the University of Virginia, Charlottesville, that a father and mother came one June day. Students had always found a welcome in this particular home. Mrs. Agnes Rothery, the wife of the professor, had written a book entitled *A Fitting Habitation,* in which she had related their unusual experiences in converting an old barn and stable into a charming little home.

Many friends who had purchased the book requested the author to autograph their copy. This father and mother called the author just as she was ready to leave for the graduating exercises, asking if they might drop by and have her autograph a copy. Even though she was in quite a hurry, something prompted her to grant their request.

Listen to her tell about the interview, and as she does, think of similar opportunities that you may have almost any day, which—if properly used—may bring joy and happiness to some individual.

I waited in our doorway until a Montana car appeared and a prettily dressed woman and a tall man with a tanned and tired face got out. They were a typical American middle-aged couple, obviously prosperous but quite unpretentious. They introduced themselves as Mr. and Mrs. Graham.

When I had greeted them and led them into the living room they stood for a moment quite still and frankly surveyed the room, then went over to the open door and looked out into the garden. Their scrutiny was so absorbed that in spite of my impatience I let a few moments pass without speaking.

Finally the man turned to me and handed me a copy of my book. "My wife and I would appreciate it if you would write your name in it," he said. "Our son often told us about coming to your charming house, and we wanted to see it ourselves."

"We have spent all day going over the University," added his wife. "We have seen Jack's room, and the library, the athletic grounds, his classrooms—everything."

"What would you like me to write in the book?" I asked patiently, taking up my pen.

"Just his name—Jack Graham—and yours, if you please," said the man.

I did this and handed him the book, wondering

nervously how much longer they would linger, and
wondering why they seemed so reluctant to take their
leave.

"Is your son graduating?" I asked.

"Our son would have graduated today," said the
man in his quiet voice. "He was killed a year ago at
Saipan."

"So we came to attend his Commencement, to see
all the places here that he loved so much—especially
your home," said the woman.

Now it was I who had not a word to say. Tears
came to my eyes and rolled down my cheeks. I
gulped awkwardly and said, "Here I am crying, and you
two are perfectly calm!"

"We—we finished our crying a long time ago," said
the woman simply.

I was still blinded with tears as I walked with them
to their car, but it was with steady voices that they
thanked me again and said good-bye.

As I watched the car move down the drive I could
picture them in the amphitheater, looking down at the
dark-capped heads of the graduating class packed in the
front rows. They would see the long line pass slowly
up to the platform where each student would receive
his diploma. They would watch it all with dry eyes,
and although the line would be closely filled they
would see one place in it which was empty.

Then suddenly, like a violent physical impact, a
terrible thought gripped me:

What if, when I had answered the telephone, *I had
said "No!"* [1]

With this story mirrored on your heart, will you get out your Bible and read again the account of the prodigal son, as recorded in Luke 15? As he returned home, not knowing how he would be received by his father, what would have been the result if the father had refused to forgive and welcome him back? You and I have a Savior who will never say "No" whenever we make a request of him. It is true that all of our requests through prayer may not always be answered as we think they should, but the answer is always for our best interest.

The Christmas season should be the happiest time of the year for every true Christian. It is the season during which we are made more conscious of the coming of our Savior to help and bless the world. As the Christmas story is read from Luke's Gospel, I wonder if we have ever stopped and asked the question, What if the keeper of the inn had not said "No" as Joseph and Mary came to Bethlehem seeking a place in which to spend the night? Had he given them a room in that humble inn. it would today be a shrine to which pilgrims would travel from all parts of the world. But the innkeeper, like so many individuals today, refused to make a place for the world's greatest personality. How many of us, day after day, are refusing to let Jesus come in and abide in our hearts?

When Jesus approached the invalid man who lay on one of the porches at the pool of Bethesda, what if the Master had refused the request which the man made? Time and time again others had refused to help him. He was without friends, and in the rush of the crowd, when the waters were troubled by the coming of an angel, he had never been able to get into the pool. But Jesus, out of his warm heart of helpfulness, said to the man, "Rise, take up thy bed, and walk." May we remember that Jesus is always ready to help.

Think now of Peter and John as they went up to the Temple to pray. At the gate they found a lame man, begging alms. As they looked upon this pitiable human being, Peter spoke the immortal words: "Silver and gold have I none; but such as I have give I thee: In the name of Jesus Christ of Nazareth rise up and walk" (Acts 3:6). Suppose they had passed him by. What if they had said "No"? He would never have known the power of their healing.

You know the tragedy of the rich young ruler's refusal to accept the invitation of the Master. In his spirit of pride and haughtiness, backed by his immense wealth, the young man said "No" to the Master. What if he had said "Yes"? He might have become as great a Christian as the apostle Paul, but he refused the invitation of Jesus. Are we doing what we should to win to Christ the scores who by their indifference and unbelief are saying "No" to him every day? How can we refuse to explain the way of salvation to them?

Shouldn't we think a long, long time before we answer "No" to the opportunities of service in our churches and Sunday schools, in our daily walk of life, and in our places of business? All about us there are individuals who need our help.

> If we could hear, as we pass along,
> The minor chords in our brother's song;
> If we could read
> The blotted lines in his once-fair creed,
> Would we not try
> To lift him up, ere we passed him by?

As we journey on, if we could know
How tired the feet that come and go;
If we could see
The heavy burdens borne patiently—
I wonder, friend,
If we would not pause some aid to lend.

In our busy haste if we could see
The heart that bleeds for our sympathy;
If we could guess
How utter our brother's loneliness,
Would we not stay
To cheer him a little on his way?

If we but knew of the bitter tears,
Of sorrows borne through the weary years,
Would we not be
A bit more kind in our ministry?
When hearts are sad,
A bit more eager to make them glad?

A solemn charge is the life we bear;
Fleeting it is, but it may be fair,
If we but heed
The outstretched hands and the hearts that plead
And day by day
Strew deeds of kindness along their way.

—*Author unknown*

18. Some Measures of Greatness

Stopping for breakfast at a restaurant out West, we were attracted by the notation on the bottom of the menu card: "Each morning I turn to the sports page of my daily paper to learn of man's achievements. Then, I turn to the front page to learn of his failures.

We all have our heroes in the athletic world, and we are anxious to read what they have done the day before. Many of them are worthy of acclaim. In contrast, the sensational news of crime and the failure of some esteemed political or business leader always make front-page headlines.

In June, 1957, a six-year-old boy had been rescued from a well in Manorville, New York, after over twenty-three hours of heroic work on the part of his rescuers. Five weeks later, angry bitterness corroded the great human drama of his rescuers when the parents received a bill for $1,500 from the doctor who had rendered modest service in perhaps saving the lad's life. There was certainly no measure of greatness on the part of this doctor.

Many inspirational speakers at luncheon clubs and church meetings frequently make use of the word "great" to mention some prominent individual in the community. They also speak of the "great" days in which we live, the "great" past we have had, the "great" opportunities we enjoy, and the "great" future we face.

There can be little doubt that we use the word "great" to excess. What do we really mean when we use it? We must not confuse the world's idea of greatness with the true Christian idea of that quality. For if notoriety, esteem, honor, and fame are the only marks of a great person, then our list of the great would encompass mostly those who are wealthy, those who are in the public eye, or those who have what the world calls glamor.

When George Washington's birthday came around in February, 1968, Henry J. Taylor, a nationally known newspaper columnist, paid a worthy tribute to a great soul. Said he: "Great men are a small family on this earth. The great fact about George Washington was his character. It was the peculiar genius of Washington and the atmosphere his character created that let loose the genius of the other men around him—the immortal circles of our founding fathers. General Robert E. Lee's father, Washington's neighbor and a hero under his command, was chosen to deliver the funeral oration when he coined the undying words, 'First in war, first in peace, and first in the hearts of his countrymen.' "

George Washington's unselfishness was the key to this. And it is a great compliment to our country that across a period of time the United States has always awarded palms— "First in the hearts of our countrymen—to selfless leaders."

Unselfishness alone has not been sufficient, of course, but in the final verdict hasn't America's unstinted accolade gone only to such men? In what other nation has this been true? Unselfishness is indeed a mark of greatness.

In evaluating the world's idea of greatness, Shakespeare had a good grasp when he observed: "Some are born great, some achieve greatness, and some have greatness thrust upon them." But Emerson was nearer the Christian idea of greatness when he wrote: "He is great who confers the most benefits."

On the lawn of the post office in a little Ontario town, there is a monument honoring a physician. It has been erected in honor of a man who had served for fifty years in the spirit of Christlikeness as a family doctor to the neighborhood. The inscription did not claim that the doctor became rich or famous as a result of the practice of his profession—it simply said that for two generations he had been at the service of that community in its time of greatest need. He lost himself in service and forgot himself into immortality.

We can all be like this doctor when we obey the admonition of our Savior: "Whosoever will save his life shall lose it; and whosoever will lose his life for my sake shall find it" (Matt. 16:25). The farmer and the fisherman, the merchant and the manufacturer, the butcher and the baker, the candlestick maker—all can be great in the same class with the humble doctor. Any useful work, well and cheerfully done in Christ's spirit, makes a worthwhile contribution to the common good.

In judging the world's idea of greatness, I would not for a moment contend that the world may not applaud its own heroes or lavish praise on those in all walks of life. I am merely saying that Christians must never lose perspective in evaluating greatness. Most of all, we must strive to impart true Christian values to our children and young people, teaching them the truth concerning greatness. We must not let the world's idea of greatness blot out what Jesus taught.

Our Lord sought to emphasize the ideal of greatness on the occasion of the Lord's Supper. He rebuked the pride and jealousy of the disciples when they again debated who would be greatest. He again repeated his formula: "He that is greatest among you, let him be as the younger; and he that is chief, as he that doth serve" (Luke 22:26).

Jesus taught greatness in one word—*service*. That person is greatest who serves others.

Charles and William Mayo of Rochester, Minnesota, have been symbolic of many who have made their lives blessings to others. These two doctors dedicated themselves to the relief of human suffering and for years performed from fifteen to thirty operations a day. Dale Carnegie described their service when they were both living: "Paupers and bank presidents, farmers and movie stars all have taken their turns in the waiting room and all were treated alike. . . . One third of their work was charity. They never sued for bills, they never took notes, and they never permitted a man to mortgage his home in order to pay them. . . . They didn't care for fame; yet they became the most famous surgeons in the United States. Their sole desire was to aid suffering humanity."

One may be born to fame or fortune; the coincidence of life may bring a person renown; but true greatness is achieved. The world can more easily afford to lose larger contributions of its greatest men than the lesser contributions of its humble men, for humility is a mark of greatness.

On a bright fall day in 1943, two young ladies were riding through the countryside and noticed a bloodmobile parked in front of a consolidated school. Immediately they decided that was an opportunity for them to donate a pint of blood. As they entered the building, an attractive structure, they noticed an elderly man. He was dressed in coveralls, carrying a bucket of water and was walking down the corridor. Thinking him to be the school janitor, they remarked: "You surely have a beautiful school. You must enjoy working here." He replied: "No, I am just helping the nurses. You see, I am a Greek, and my country is at war. This is the only service I can render." They complimented him on his devotion to his country.

That night they had tickets to the Minneapolis Symphony. It was time for the program to begin, and the conductor of the orchestra approached the podium. The same little grey-haired man was the leader, Demetrio Metropolis, the world-wide acclaimed musician. Even though he had reached the peak of his musical career, he was humble enough to render a modest service for others in need. Humility is indeed a mark of greatness.

Courage, modesty, honesty, truthfulness—these are only a few signs of greatness. We may be led to achieve Christian greatness when we see how much the world needs Christian service. This is a hungry, anxious, Christless world. The Christian is great who uses his life for God, a life that has been given him and the opportunities life affords him for the service of others.

19. Facing Life's Storms

Today, adverse circumstances and the world situation are pounding some people to pieces emotionally. There is a feeling of grave uneasiness in the world. Many people in our own country live in dread of what the morrow may bring forth. We are living in a day of trouble, and trouble is a touchstone which tests the quality of human character. If there was ever a time when men and women needed inner resources of quietness and confidence, it is in these days.

Time, the usual panacea, does not change the situation. In fact, each day seems to increase the difficulties. Where can we find help? God is the same yesterday, today, and forever. That does not mean that God is static, but it does mean that he is unchangeable. "It is of the Lord's mercies that we are not consumed, because his compassions fail not. They are new every morning; great is they faithfulness. The Lord is my portion, saith my soul; therefore will I hope in him. The Lord is good unto them that wait for him, to the soul that seeketh him" (Lam. 3:22-25).

Washington Irving relates that in every true human heart there is a spark of heavenly fire which may be invisible in the broad daylight of prosperity but which kindles up and blazes in the dark hour of adversity. Wherever such persons are to be found, they are a steadying force to less stable lives. This is one of the contributions that true religion, a dedicated heart, invariably makes. It keeps us cool and unafraid when others falter. It imparts to us a courage so great that those who lack it look like weaklings. A radiant faith in the day of trouble will lift us high above any misgivings and fear, and it will make us rallying points at which others, who have grown frightened and lost heart, will become brave again.

There are these radiant Christians in almost every community. A pastor tells of one in his congregation, one of the most winsome and attractive women he had ever known. She had the gift to understand those who came into her presence, and somehow left something of herself with them. When the opportunity came to talk with her alone, he said: "Would you allow me to make a personal inquiry? Have you ever gone through some unusual suffering?"

"It is strange that you should ask," she replied. "A few years ago I lost a little baby. You will never know the agony and suffering I endured. I thought I would die myself. But God took that cross and taught me how to use it for others. Otherwise, I would have shriveled up."

So that was her secret. Beauty from suffering! It happens time and again. When you meet a person with unusual poise and beauty of character, you may almost take it for granted that somewhere in the past he has walked through "the valley of the shadow of death." We have such a couple in our own church. In the summer of 1971, as they backed their car out of the driveway, their eighteen-month-old boy had hidden under the car, falling asleep. He was crushed to death. There are not two more radiant, dedicated Christians in our church membership. "But the God of all grace, who hath called us unto his eternal glory by Christ Jesus, after that ye have suffered a while, make you perfect, stablish, strengthen, settle you. To him be glory and dominion for ever and ever" (1 Pet. 5:10).

God still speaks through every tragedy. Every person and every nation can learn unforgettable lessons in God's school of adversity. It is only when the sky is darkest that the stars shine more brightly.

Some of life's most radiant blessings come out of wounding. Wheat must be crushed to be bread. The candle must burn itself up to give light. The ground must be broken with a sharp plough before it is ready to receive the seed. The finest china in the world is burned at least three times. We can learn from tragedy either defeat or victory. A poem by an anonymous author expresses this truth with clarity: "Two men looked out through prison bars, One saw the mud, the other saw the stars."

Boating these days is a popular sport, especially on the many man-made lakes. Most of these boats are motorized, yet the old-fashioned sailboats are still used in many areas, especially off the coasts of New England and elsewhere. An avid sportsman tells how, when sailing in a brisk breeze in the Atlantic some ten miles off shore, he was lying on the deck enjoying the sun and sea air. Looking aloft, he happened to see a weak house wren perched on the rigging between the masts. He had no idea how it got there, but he presumed it may have been a bit confused, blown seaward in the strong wind, and dismayed to find no comforting tree or other landing spot in the midst of the white-capped waves. Sea gulls can soar indefinitely over the waters, and ride on their surface—but the tiny house wren—amid circumstances that were too much for it—needed, and fortunately found, something to cling to in its necessity.

Life is often like that. Circumstances almost overwhelm us. We are perplexed, dismayed and wearied, and in our distress we need something firm to which we may hold fast. "What do you do when there is a bad storm?" a lad asked his father, who was driving the boat when they were out on the lake. The father would always point to a compass near him and say, "When the fog sets in or when the storm comes, I can always rely on this."

What do we do in the middle of life's storms? All of us will have them sooner or later. Do we have a compass in which we have confidence? In our human frailty we need a guide, one whose ability is beyond our own. Cling fast to the Master's hand which is ready to guide you. Let him be your compass in the storms of life. "Come unto me, all ye that labour and are heavy laden, and I will give you rest. Take my yoke upon you, and learn of me; for I am meek and lowly in heart; and ye shall find rest unto your souls" (Matt. 11:28-29).

Have you ever thought about how the Lord is always with you and how he can bring you safely through any experience? Too many of us forget it. A surgical magazine tells the story of a hard-pressed, irritable, nervous, overworked surgeon in a New York hospital. He was ready to perform an emergency operation, but he was in a hurry—there were other operations to perform that day.

They wheeled in the patient—a beautiful girl of seventeen—seriously injured in an accident. She had not been told that she was probably a hopeless case. The nurse who was to administer the anesthetic stood over her and said kindly: "Relax. Breathe deeply, and you will forget the pain."

The girl looked up to the nurse and said: "Would you

mind very much if I first repeated something my mother taught me when I was a little girl? I would like to say Psalm 23."

The nurse looked at the doctor. He nodded, and the girl began: "The Lord is my shepherd; I shall not want."

The surgeon continued his preparations, but everyone else stood silent, listening. They had heard these wonderful words in church many times, but they never sounded so moving before. Here they had another meaning—a meaning of a deeper kind.

The girl went on: "Though I walk through the valley of the shadow of death, I will fear no evil; for thou art with me." The nurse held the cone above her to begin the anesthetic.

"Hold it," the surgeon said. "Let her finish." Then he spoke to the girl: "Go on, honey, say it to the end. And say it for me, too, won't you?"

They all listened as her heart full of faith filled that operating room with some of the most moving words ever written. The doctor looked down at her. He relaxed, his sense of irritation gone. There was no feeling of other duties pressing him. His patient was at peace and ready for him. Everyone in that room was lifted by the girl's faith. How could an operation performed under such conditions not be a success?

There is more and better therapy in faith than in anything else in the whole world. If you will fill yourself with it, there is nothing you need ever fear.

Despite the murky bewilderment of these fast-changing days, let us go forward with purpose more thoughtfully brave and with faith more sacrificially confident than ever before. May we be enabled to think clearly and always with straightforward integrity.

If we must sometimes be called upon to travel some lonely road far into the gloomy night; if we must feel the dull ache of some hurt of yesterday or must walk in the hush of some trying ordeal today or tomorrow; if we must sometimes be misunderstood and eat the bread of sorrow and dwell in the house of pain—may we be given the faith that can triumphantly go alone in the dark, the love that suffers long and is kind, the hope that grows brighter and stronger unto the perfect day, always remembering that we can "come boldly unto the throne of grace, that we may obtain mercy, and find grace to help in time of need" (Heb. 14:16).

"If thou faint in the day of adversity, thy strength is small" (Prov. 24:10).

20. Untarnished Loyalty

It was the great emancipator, Abraham Lincoln, who once said, "I am not bound to win, but I am bound to be true. I am not bound to succeed, but I am bound to live by the light that I have. I must stand with anybody that stands right, stand with him while he is right, and part with him when he is wrong."

And it was William Shakespeare who wrote:

"To thine own self be true,
And it may follow, as the night the day.
Thou canst not then be false to any man."

After the death of Moses, God had another noble servant ready to lead his people, the Israelites, on their pilgrimage into the promised land. The book of Joshua records this dramatic history. God was constantly speaking to Joshua, giving him instructions and counsel.

Joshua made a special point to remind them of the manifold blessings which were theirs from the hand of a gracious God. In doing so, he admonished them: "But take diligent heed to do the commandment and the law, which Moses the servant of the Lord charged you, to love the Lord your God, and to walk in all his ways, and to keep his commandments, and to cleave unto him, and to serve him with all your heart and with all your soul" (Josh. 22:5). He was demanding untarnished loyalty of the people he was leading.

Throughout his teachings, Jesus was constantly proclaiming the necessity of loyalty and devotion to his heavenly Father. In the Sermon on the Mount, as he was setting forth the law of riches as related to the kingdom, he said: "No man can serve two masters; for either he will hate the one, and love the other; or else he will hold to the one, and despise the other. Ye cannot serve God and mammon" (Matt. 6:24).

And again, after he had healed the demoniac, he heard the Pharisees questioning his authority to heal by the power of God. He said: "Every kingdom divided against itself is brought to desolation; and every city or house divided against itself shall not stand" (Matt. 12:25). And in the same discussion, he said: "He that is not with me is against me; and he that gathereth not with me scattereth abroad" (Matt. 12:30).

In government and in business, loyalty is a prime requisite for employment. When an official of city, state, or national government is sworn into office, there are ceremonies whereby the elected official pledges his allegiance and loyalty to the government of which he is to become a servant. Another beautiful and meaningful ceremony is that of the Pledge of Allegiance to the flag of our country. If this is true in these areas of life, how much more important is it that every true Christian should daily witness to his love for and loyalty to God.

Though best known for his novels, A. J. Cronin has also written a number of short stories and vignettes. One of the

most challenging and heart-warming of these miniatures is
"A Candle in Vienna," written after World War I, following
his first visit to the once-beautiful city. For weeks he had
looked forward to visiting the place, which in the past, he
had known and loved so much. But as the plane landed,
his mood had grown progressively bitter as he saw at close
hand the utter destruction which the Germans had wrought.
Even his hotel room was sparsely furnished and unheated
for mid-winter.

In the early afternoon he set out in the cutting wind on
his tour of inspection, passed the shattered cathedral and
the ruins of the opera house in which he had listened with
happiness to the great music of famous opera personalities.
He had come prepared for material destruction, for shattered houses, heaps of rubble of bombed buildings. But he
had not foreseen the empty, silent hopelessness that per-
vaded the gray and dingy streets.

Blind anger grew within him, a sullen resentment against
a Providence that would allow such things come to pass.
Added to this was the personal discomfort as the February
twilight fell and it began to rain, a heavy, freezing sleet
that threatened to penetrate even his fairly warm clothing.
He sought shelter in a small church which had escaped destruction. It was empty and almost dark, except for the
faint flicker of the sanctuary light. Impatiently, he sat down
to wait for the worst of the downpour to pass.

"Suddenly, I heard footsteps and, turning, I saw an old
man enter the church. He wore no coat, and his tall figure,
gaunt and stiffly erect, clad in a thin and much mended
suit, was painfully shabby. As he advanced toward the side
altar, I observed with surprise that he was carrying in his
arms a child, a little girl of about six, dressed in the garments

of poverty. When he reached the railing of the altar, he put her down gently. I perceived then, from the helpless movement of her limbs, that she was paralyzed. Still supporting her with great patience, he encouraged her to kneel, arranging her hands so that she could cling to the altar rail. When he had succeeded, he smiled at her, as though congratulating her on her achievement. Then he knelt, spare and erect, beside her.

"For a few minutes they remained thus, then the old man rose. I heard the thin echo of a small coin falling into the box, then saw him take a candle, light it, and give it to the child. She held it in one transparent hand for a long moment while the glow cast a little halo around her, making visible the pleased expression on her pale, pinched features. Then she placed the candle upright on the small iron stand before the shadowed altar, admiring her little gift, dedicating it with the rapt upturned tilt of her head.

"Presently the old man got up again and, lifting the child, began to carry her in his arms out of the church. All the time that I had watched them I felt myself intruding on their privacy, guilty of a sort of sacrilege. Yet now, though that feeling remained, an irresistable impulse made me rise and follow them to the church porch.

"Here, drawn to one side, was a small homemade conveyance—a rickety wooden box with lopsided sticks for shafts, mounted on the two old perambulator wheels which had long ago lost their rubber tires. Into this equipage the old man was bestowing the child, spreading an old potato sack across her limbs. Now that I stood close to them, I could plainly confirm what I had already suspected. Every line of the old man's drawn face, the cropped mustache, the fine nose, the proud eyes under deep brows showed him a true aristocrat, one of those patrician Viennese, though no fault of his own, the war had brought utter ruin. The child, whose peaked features resembled his own, was almost certainly his grandaughter. As with his veined, fine hands he finished tucking the sack around her, he glanced at me. A rush of questions was on my tongue, but something, the spiritual quality of that face, restrained my curiosity. I could only say, with awkardness, 'It is cold.'

"He answered politely, 'Less cold than it has been this winter.'

"There was a pause. My gaze turned to the child whose blue eyes were fixed upon us. 'The war,' I said, still looking at her.

" 'Yes, the war,' he answered. 'The same bomb killed her mother and father.'

"Another, and a longer pause.

" 'You come here often?' I regretted this crudity immediately when it escaped me. But he took no offense.

" 'Yes, every day, to pray.' He smiled faintly. 'And also to show the good God we are not angry with him.'

"I could find no reply. And as I stood in the silence he straightened, buttoned his jacket, picked up the shafts of the little buggy and with a faint smile, that polite inclination of his head, moved off with the child into the gathering darkness.

"No sooner were they gone than I had again an insufferable desire to pursue them. I wanted to help, to offer them money, to strip off my warm coat, to do something impetuous and spectacular. But I remained rooted to the spot. I knew that this was no case of common charity, that something which I could give would be refused. Instead it was they who had given me something. They who had lost everything refused to despair; they could still believe. A feeling of confusion rose in me. Now there was no anger in my heart, no concern for my own petty deprivation, but only pity and a pervading sense of shame.

"The rain had gone off. But I did not go out. I hesitated. Then I turned and went back toward the faithful beacon which still burned at the side altar in the no longer empty church. One candle in a ruined city. But while it shone, there seemed hope for the world." [1]

Loyalty to God is fundamental. Feelings, words, deeds must be beads strung on the string of duty. Let the world tell you in a hundred ways what your life is for. Say you ever and only, "Lo, I come to do thy will, O my God." Out of that beautiful root grows the beautiful life, the life radically and radiantly true to God—the only life that can be lived in both worlds. The only life that can demonstrate the spirit of love and compassion as demonstrated by the Good Samaritan.

21. Today Is a Gift

Few of us know the value of a day—a twenty-four-hour day—until it is taken from us. It was Voltaire who, having spent a life of blasphemy, whispered to his physician as he neared the end: "I will give all my fortune if you'll give me six months more to live."

And it was Ralph Waldo Emerson who stated: "Write it on your heart that every day is the best day of the year. He is rich who owns the day, and no one owns the day who allows it to be invaded with fret and anxiety. Finish every day and be done with it. You have done what you could. Some blunders and absurdities, no doubt, crept in. Forget them as soon as you can. Tomorrow is a new day. Begin it well and serenely, without too high a spirit to be encumbered with your old nonsense. This new day is too dear, with hopes and invitations, to waste a moment on the yesterdays."

How our lives would be changed if we determined to live each day to the fullest. Full of love for those in our family circles, full of concern for those less fortunate than ourselves, full of sympathy for those in sorrow. A busy pastor, almost to the state of exhaustion from his heavy load of responsibility, was asking for guidance. As out of the clear blue, the Lord seemed to say to him: "Live twenty-four hours at the time. Fill each day with me." And the psalmist has said: "It is a good time to give thanks unto the Lord and to sing praises unto thy name, O most high; to shew forth thy loving-kindness in the morning, and thy faithfulness every day" (Ps. 92:1-2).

In *Look* magazine of December 6, 1968, astronaut Walt Cunningham turned philosopher: "Between the time of our arrival on this earth and the time you depart, there are many ways of living. I believe the worst way is to exist as a miser spends his money, clinging to life and paying it out in dear little segments. The true way to live is to spend your life generously, invest yourself in it . . . It is not how long you live, but how you spend your life." Too many of us dribble away our days with no real purpose. Did not the Master say: "For whosoever will save his life shall lose it: and whosoever will lose his life for my sake shall find it. For what is a man profited, if he shall gain the whole world and lose his own soul? Or what shall a man give in exchange for his soul?" (Matt. 16:25-26).

Every day brings its problems, its decisions, its changes. Wouldn't it be wonderful if you only had to be concerned about what happens today? If only you could forget what transpired yesterday, and if you only didn't have to worry about what tomorrow may bring, life would be simple. There would be one day only to merit your attention and energies.

After all, anybody can gather up enough strength to tackle the problems of today or can muster will power to resist temptation. It is when we add the weight of those eternities, yesterday and tomorrow, that we collapse or become depressed. No point of lamenting over the opportunities we missed yesterday, for they are gone forever. No use of becoming paralyzed for fear of what tomorrow may bring, for most of the things we worry about never do come to pass or are beyond our control.

But today, that's different! God will give me enough power to be triumphant for today. He will not test me beyond what I am able to bear this day, but he will provide the strength to see me through. No need, therefore, to worry about yesterday or tomorrow.

Some go into a day and miss everything. As though its fruits are hidden underneath some dense foliage. But there are others who enter every day expecting great things, go after them, and get many that they never dreamed of getting. For each new day there is a tremendous amount of surprise. It looks quite the same as every day, but in reality it is all new; every day is a virgin field for work and new achievements, new opportunities for doing good.

As each new day dawns and you go forth, do what you can to make this earth a cleaner, brighter place. Do what you can to put a smile upon a frowning face. Do what you can to put things right when everything looks wrong—turning clouds into sunshine and the discords into song. Never lose a chance to light the lamp of charity or to speak a cheery word of hope and sympathy. Try to be a Good Samaritan.

Make this a well-spent day. Don't invest your precious hours in things that bear no fruit; silly pastimes, foolish aims, and pleasure's vain pursuit. Go about the business of God's kingdom upon earth. Let your life proclaim your creed. Let all you say and do testify to what you are. All of us must render an account, and no one knows the day when we will be called upon to give it.

Remember, every day is a gift from God. Spend this

God-sent day caught up in things worthwhile. Fashion something beautiful wherever you may be. Don't let ugliness and drabness be your lot. Though your means be limited and the place you may live be humble, introduce a touch of color, artistry, grace. Ugly things depress the spirit and offend the eye. Always do your utmost to improve and to beautify. Even though your efforts seem to leave no lasting trace, never lose the chance to make the world a sweeter place. Weave at least one golden thread through every day you live. Stamp out every spark of hatred and kindle love instead.

Someone has said, "Today is the first day of the rest of your life." When one of the psalmists declared: "This is the day the Lord has made, we will rejoice and be glad in it," he was being a great psychologist. He knew through actual experience that an individual can be happy if he lives "today" in all its beauty and fullness. He felt that since we do not know what tomorrow will present, it is impractical to worry about it. If we live our best today, the chances are that tomorrow will bring good rather than bad. The psalmist knew that "yesterday cannot be recalled; tomorrow cannot be assured; only today is ours." On an attractive correspondence card we found these words:

> Yesterday is but a memory.
> Tomorrow is an unchartered course.
> So live today so it will be
> A memory without remorse.

Remember, today is a gift from God. Use it well. As each day dawns, we don't know what it holds for us of good or ill, what pains and problems it may bring to try the nerve and test the will. But somehow, by some miracle, the necessary strength is found to do our duties and to bear the burdens of the daily round.

God does not make demands on us beyond our own capacity. He knows our limitations and knows what we can do and be. In the darkest hours, there always comes a star to guide, a light to lead. Hope and help are given us and, in faith, according to our need. "The Lord upholdeth the righteous" (Ps. 37:17).

Today is a gift!

NOTES

Chapter 1
1. A Purnell Bailey. Board of Higher Education and Ministry, Washington, D. C. Used by permission.

Chapter 2
Wilfred A. Peterson. *The Art of Living* (New York: Simon and Schuster, 1960), pp. 8-9. Used by permission.

Chapter 3
1. Howard A Rusk. *Random House and The Reader's Digest Condensed Books,* Pleasantville, N. Y. Used by permission.

Chapter 7
1 Ralph McGill. "The Stamp of Genuine Love," *The Atlanta Constitution,* October 12, 1967. Used by permission.

Chapter 8
1. James Keller. *One Moment Please* (Garden City, N. Y., The Christophers, Inc., Doubleday and Co., 1950). Used by permission.

Chapter 9

1. "The Gifts of Gregory Menn," *Reader's Digest.*
August, 1970, pp. 108-12. Adapted and used by permission.

Chapter 10

1. Adapted from *Guideposts,* Guideposts Associates. May,
1964, pp. 3-4. Used by permission.

Chapter 11

1. *Reader's Digest,* July, 1946, p. 87. Used by permission.

Chapter 17

1. "What If I Had Said No," *Reader's Digest,* July, 1947.
Used by permission.

Chapter 20

1. A. J. Cronin, "A Candle in Vienna." *The Word Lives
On.* Edited by Frances Brebtano. Doubleday and Co., New
York, 1951. Used by permission of publisher and *Reader's
Digest.* June, 1936.